I Count the Dark;

A MEMOIR OF

PERSEVERANCE, **T**RAUMA, **S**URVIVAL AND
DETERMINATION

Berthienna E. Green

© 2023 Berthienna E. Green

Book Cover Design By: TamikaINK.com

Interior Book Design & Formatting: TamikaINK.com

Edited By: Alesha Shaw

ALL RIGHTS RESERVED. No part of this book may be reproduced in any written, electronic, recording, or photocopying without written permission of the publisher or author. The exception would be in the case of brief quotations embodied in the critical articles or reviews and pages where permission is specifically granted by the publisher or author.

LEGAL DISCLAIMER. Although the author has made every effort to ensure that the information in this book was correct at press time, the author does not assume and at this moment disclaim any liability to any party for any loss, damage, or disruption caused by errors or omissions, whether such errors or omissions result from negligence, accident, or any other cause.

Published By: Tamika INK

Library of Congress Cataloging – in- Publication Data has been applied for.

ISBN: 979-8-9881046-0-5

PRINTED IN THE UNITED STATES OF AMERICA.

Praise for
"I Count The Dark"

"Truly a work of art captivating and gripping. A book that had me from the first word to the last. A riveting story, an artistic way of telling a tragedy. Thank you for such a great read."
Cassendre Gibbs
Nurse Practitioner, YouTuber 'Tee Times Casse'
@teetimecasse6869

"I Count the Dark is a powerful memoir of perseverance. In having the courage to share her story, others who've experienced Military Sexual Trauma (MST) will know that they are not alone, and it is never too late to seek help. We can all move from victim to survivor to thriver! Thank you, Tina, for being a beacon of light, illuminating a way forward for fellow veterans, and championing change." —-
Susan Alden
Army Veteran & Fellow "Thriver"
Founder of Mind Body Aloha Wellness
www.mindbodyaloha.com

"I Count the Dark is a powerful retelling of the rape and trauma experienced by a young woman from my hometown, Philadelphia, PA. Berthienna gives an authentic voice to the epidemic of military sexual assault plaguing every branch of the United States military. Her triumphant story of survival 40 years after being victimized by one of the most "trusted" systems in America is a must-read."

Crystal
Friend and Neighbor

"A fascinating, honest, and well-written read from the very beginning. Tina has a way of writing that draws you in, as though you were right there experiencing life with her."

T. Anthony-Horton
Author of 'Office Antics & Sexual Liaisons'-available on Amazon

----

"Wow! This book is a powerful story about sexual trauma and the toll that post-traumatic stress has on one's life. For anyone, such as myself, who has questioned a victim's behavior before and after an assault, this book clearly explains it. "

Joyce Williams
Lifelong Friend

"What a heroic act of courage is *I Count The Dark*. Green speaks aloud the traumas she endured in noble pursuit of service to her country, not on the battlefield but in the barracks. But this is a story of the light as much as the dark. In her pursuit of justice and healing, and in telling her story, she provides a beacon of hope for all survivors."

Anne Dubuisson

"This book is a must read! Tina's compelling story of her horrific life experience in the United States Air Force is long overdue. There are countless others, mainly women, who have had similar experiences, reported and unreported. Sadly, the perpetrators go unpunished. No one should ever have to endure such pain, violence, and senseless microaggression for reporting predatory acts of sexual aggression. Where is justice equality? I believe "My encounters with uncivilized men" is probably a more appropriate title for this literary work. Well done, Tina. Thank you for your service. Thank you for standing up and being strong.

Dr. Theodore B. Terry
Researcher, Educator, Father, and Friend.

Dedication

---~~∽⊙⊙~~---

This book is dedicated to my mother, Ruth Green Reed, the woman who helped shape me into the warm, loving, grateful person that I am today.

Also, to my four wonderful, beautiful, talented, and loving children, Brandon, Evelyn, Ralph, and Genevieve, you are my reasons for living,

And the absolute bestest friend anyone could ever have, Sheila Peterson, a strong, black woman from B-More, aka Baltimore, Maryland, whom I met in 1996 and who continues to be one of my strongest advocates to this day.

Acknowledgments

My story is true, but I have changed some names and locations to protect the privacy of others.

I have known for quite some time that this memoir could not have been written without reflecting on the love and support that I received from my mother, RuthieMae Ford-Green-Reed, or 'Ruthie' as she was called by her family growing up, and later everyone just stuck to calling her, Ruth. Although she has passed on to glory, I remember her smooth, soft skin and the scent of Jergens lotion on her skin which I could smell every time she passed by. That smell would produce an instant smile on my face because I was so glad to see her and knew that soon she would plant a great big kiss on my cheek and surround me with a warm hug. Thank you, mama Ruth; you were always my biggest and strongest supporter and cheerleader.

To the bestest big brother in the whole wide world, I hope you know that you have always played a strong role in my life. I may have never said the words out loud but know that every decision that I make begins and often ends with wondering what you would have thought about it and how you might have handled it differently.

To my four handsome and beautiful children, now young adults, I appreciate how each of you stood by eagerly cheering me on to complete my college degree with many late nights and early mornings and how none of you put up too much of a fuss when I sometimes could not take you to different social and sporting events because I had to study and finish my papers. I know that parts of my story are shocking to you, but hopefully, in reading through this book, you can understand a little bit better the journey our lives have taken since all of you came into my life. I love you all deeply and dearly.

Sheila Peterson, Sheila Peterson, Sheila Peterson. What would I do without my road dog by my side thru thick and thin? You are the truest of friends, and I will always treasure you.

Finally, thank you to the many family members and friends I have met in life whose lives touched my own in such a unique and inspiring way which led me to produce this collection of my thoughts and experiences, which helped shape me into the woman I am today. Every experience, no matter the outcome, played a huge part in my development as a human being, daughter, sister, aunt, wife, mother, and friend. There are still moments when I reflect and recall a moment in my life when I would have preferred for there to have been a different outcome, but I know that to have changed the outcome would mean not being who I am and who I am is a very strong, intelligent, beautiful, loving black woman. Thank you all for touching my life in such a meaningful way.

Table of Contents

Foreword 1
Early Life In North Philly 18
Humphrey's Pills/Mama Ruth 23
WSJ Article And My First Attempt To File 34
Goodbye Philly, Hello USAF 47
Daydreaming 101 54
Duty Begins 56
No 341s for Me 68
Kat and Mason, My Besties 75
Airman Green 78
Time Keeps On Slipping 86
The 24-Hour Engagement 94
Auntie 98
Shattered Dreams 102
The Ill-Fated Invitation 105
No More Sleazeballs In My Life... Please! 110
James Wilson Green aka "Slim" 115
Did I Hear Someone Say...Complaint? 122
Military Discharge 131
What Happens In Vegas... 133
Normalcy??? 136
A Memoir? Be Careful, Tina 138
Davis – Back In Love, Again 141
The Unraveling... 147
Matthews ... My VA Guide 156
The VA Claims Process...The Beginning 165
Matthews...Returning To The Claims Process 171
Apology- No, Apology 179
Military Sexual Trauma-MST 188
Military Sexual Trauma-As Defined By The Va 191
Past...Present...Future 195
ICountTheDark 201
A Poem 201
About Berthienna E. Green 205

I COUNT THE DARK

Foreword

*I really don't think life is about the I-could-have-beens.
Life is only about the I-tried-to-do.
I don't mind the failure but I can't imagine that I'd forgive myself if I didn't try.*
Nikki Giovanni

I have always been a Solitaire player, and I learned how to play by watching my mother play for years when I was a child. I can still see Mama sitting at the dining room table, a long, slim Saratoga menthol cigarette dangling from her mouth with her head cocked to the left, spirals of smoke rising to the ceiling as she dealt the cards into precise stacks of seven so that she could turn the cards over one by one to find a match. She often played solitaire at the dining room table in her baby blue housecoat, her jet-black hair softly twisted into a lazy updo.

She focused so intently on those cards, quietly alternating sips of gin with a drag on her cigarette and the soft tap of the cards on the dining room table.

I would sit quietly by her side, watching her play for hours, just enjoying our time together. Mama never spoke to me when I sat beside her, and sometimes it was almost as if I wasn't even there, as if I was invisible and she had the house all to herself. The only sound was the smack of the cards on the table as she slid them into place. She would play as long as she could, sometimes for hours, before life interrupted her thoughts. Then in one swift move, she would suddenly wave her left hand like a wand all across the table, gather all the cards, and in seconds she was done for the day. She would open the box, tilt back the flap, and slide the *cards into the box in one swift move, and suddenly, before I knew it, I was on the receiving end of one of her brightest smiles as she pulled me into the warmest and sweetest smelling hug. I would sit by her side for hours, just waiting for her to finish so that I could be on the receiving end of her joy.*

I realize now that it was in those moments that I gained the strength I would need to handle some of the difficulties that life would throw at me, and also learned how to channel my energies into a healing force that would lift me up out of my misery. Mama used that time while she played solitaire as her form of meditation and reflection. I noticed that whenever she was stressed or struggling to figure out how to feed and care for a family of seven children that those were the moments when I saw her turn inward, looking for solutions. Then there were also the times when I would hear her praying long into the night when she thought everyone was asleep, asking God for his grace and mercy to help her through a difficult time.

Mama learned how to pray from Grandma Bertha and when the two of them prayed together, I always felt so much better. That only happened on rare occasions, mostly because we didn't live with my grandmother by the time all seven of us came into the world, but I can still remember hearing them pray when we all went to church together. BerthaMae may not have approved of Mama having so many children out of wedlock, but no matter how we came into this world, she definitely loved Mama and all of us, too, and would spend many days praying over us and helping Mama as much as she could. The many strengths I learned from my mother have molded and shaped me into the strong woman I am today, and I thank God for her every day.

This is the story of how a teenage girl was plucked from the mean streets of North Philadelphia to be planted into the dry, barren desert sands of Abilene, Texas. She knew nothing of what was to come, nor did she know how drastically her

I COUNT THE DARK

life would change. In retrospect, it might seem as if living life on the gang-ridden streets of North Philadelphia would have been more perilous than volunteering in the United States Air Force, but that did not turn out to be the case. After all, we encounter many different kinds of danger, and perhaps it is the danger we cannot know or plan for that is the most threatening. In North Philly, I lived with my family, friends, and boyfriend, Davis, all of whom were comfortable and familiar. I was far more unprepared than I could ever know to face the dark side of life in the Air Force.

I Count the Dark covers the most difficult period of my life when I was sexually assaulted and raped while serving in the United States Airforce. I fell into many ditches while serving in the military, and my journey to salvation has been long and arduous, but I am proud to say that I came out the other side stronger and better. The writing of this book took just a little over a year from beginning to end, but it has taken me over 40 years to get to a point in my life where I was comfortable sharing my journey with you. In writing, I learned that I was stronger than I thought I was and that it was my strength that helped me make it through the toughest times. I wrote this book to help other women with similar experiences realize that you can overcome some of life's most difficult challenges with perseverance, faith, and the love of family. I pray that you can connect with my story and that it might serve as an anchor as you continue your journey to self-discovery. Learning to love me and value what I bring to the conversation has been a very important lesson learned later in life. I know the value and impact now of every step along my journey that has brought me to this point in my life. I do not know that I would be the same self-assured, charismatic, strong, and resilient woman I am today had I not labored through the violations against my character, body, and soul, the ones I am about to share with you in this book.

Dr. Justin Jackson and How I Healed

As I think back on those years, I realize now that I never categorized myself as broken; I went through life attempting to handle one situation after another as it presented itself to me at the time. Whenever a relationship failed, I blamed myself for not realizing what the man needed from me, and then I would change myself accordingly so that the next man would receive a better version of me. Whenever I failed at something at work, I set out to change certain traits within me to perform better the next time. Whenever something went wrong at home with the children and later with my husband, I would once again set out to figure out what was wrong with me and read a self-help book or watch a video that would help me to become more relatable in dealing with those situations.

In the beginning, I never fully acknowledged that I was broken because I was too busy feeling all the pain around and inside of me. By the time I came to realize how broken I was, I was already in my mid-to-late thirties and had suffered through several of what I would call mini-breakdowns, with one of my most significant breakdowns happening in the latter part of 2002. It wasn't until I started seeing a psychiatrist named Dr. Justin Jackson that I was able to realize how broken I was and came to appreciate the person I was back then in order to begin the process on my road to becoming healthy.

Dr. Justin Jackson was the very first person that I had spoken with about the drinking game "Cardinal Puff-Puff," and he knew of the game since he had served in the military as well. I believe that he served in the Air Force, but I can't recall for certain. Having someone to talk to that was familiar with some of my military experiences was extremely important. I realized in the later years that a part of me always felt like no one believed a word I said about the military because they couldn't imagine that kind of thing happening to anyone back then in the 1970s. Sometimes it seems like it was all just a horrible dream because back in the '70s we didn't believe women were routinely assaulted. Until it happened to me I never would have thought such things could happen to anyone.

Dr. Justin Jackson would continually correct me whenever I spoke about needing to be better and needing to figure out what was wrong with me when dealing with failures in my life. He would tell me to stop referring to myself as the problem and begin to just look at the situation as being the problem and not something that I needed to fix all the time. He ended every session with encouraging words, telling me to appreciate myself more and to go easy on myself because nothing is really that bad that it can't be fixed. He would also tell me that I had experienced something bad, it was in the past, and tell me to leave it in the past for now, and instead just deal with the present.

I know now that he realized that I was in no shape at that time to decipher what had happened in the past so he kept me focused on the present and helped me learn to recognize and appreciate the things that I had accomplished in life up until that point. Understanding what it took to be a mother to my children was a big part of my accomplishments, but it was something I took for granted back then. I saw it as a duty to be performed and not necessarily something to be accomplished. Being a mother contributed largely to my healing process because it took the focus off me and placed it on doing everything I could to ensure that my children were well cared for, nurtured, and loved. I thoroughly enjoyed every aspect of motherhood, bonding with my children while nursing them; taking them back and forth to the doctor's office for their checkups; registering them in school; helping them with homework and healing all of the skinned knees, drying all the tears and hurt feelings they had as they progressed through childhood into adulthood up until the time that I had to let each one go off on their own as a young adult to figure out how the world works.

Progressing in my career at the Federal Reserve Bank of Philadelphia was the other large part of my healing that I took for granted back then. I awoke every morning fixated on doing the best at my job so that I could progress from a Check Processing Clerk to a Wire Transfer Clerk, then Customer Service Analyst, and finally to creating the job description for the Associate Specialist/Coordinator of the Training & Quality Division of the Customer Services and

Support department and performing those duties at the end of my career at the Bank.

Back then, healing meant being able to perform my duties and responsibilities as a mother and a contributing member of the workforce. I was allowed time to meditate and time to celebrate birthdays and my pregnancies, and spend as much time as possible with my friends. Healing also meant understanding that I needed to take daily antidepressant medication and see my therapist regularly. Healing meant I could sit down anywhere and suddenly have a poem reveal itself to me as I was taking a bite of my sandwich while sitting outside on a bench, feeling the breeze blow through my hair. I was learning how to listen to what my mind and my body needed, which was a new experience for me.

Learning to overcome stuttering when I was younger which then led to hours of practicing how to speak properly and intelligently while articulating and enunciating every sound and syllable spoken out of my mouth. Honing and mastering my public speaking skills while growing up led me to win a Southern Las Vegas Nevada speech competition in the late 1980s when I lived in Las Vegas, Nevada after separating from the military. Learning these skills helped me immensely when the time came for me to put my thoughts down on paper in order to file a claim with the VA, as well as whenever I had to supply the VA with more information in support of my claim for benefits

I also realize now that as painful as my experiences were that I was strong enough to come through them on the other side with a stronger sense of purpose. I believe my purpose in life is to be a nurturer. To be someone who helps others realize their own strengths and helps them to see that through the midst of pain and sadness, they can realize their own strengths if they hang in there long enough and don't give in. God had a bigger purpose for my life so he wouldn't let me give up.

Hyper-encoding and Flashbacks

There was a moment after my first suicide attempt (and that word "first" is not lost on me) when I remember seeing myself writing furiously in my journal about being raped. I can feel the hardback covers, front and back of the journal. There are light blue and white clouds floating in a wonderful blue sky, and I can also see the light blue colored pages of the journal. Feeling the warm tears rushing down both sides of my face, I see myself scribbling faster and faster in my journal. The force of my hand is causing rips to appear on the page. Now I'm cussing (loudly in my mind) at the page, at the time, at space, at nothing and no one in particular other than myself for my own stupidity! *Why did I go to TSgt Alameda's house with the other airmen? How could I not have known what "choir practice" really was? No one forced me to participate, but I did it anyway.* I am crying so hard, breathing even harder, writing, and writing and writing, and words are almost incoherent. I could no longer see through the tears streaming down my face. In a final fit of rage, I tossed the book across the room and just fell out on my bunk in frustration. I figured no one heard a single word out of my mouth because I had stifled every emotion and spilled it all out underneath my breath through clenched teeth. When experiencing a flashback, it's as if you're instantly removed from your present existence and miraculously transplanted to that other time and place, so even though this memory is occurring years after the fact, all it took was me reading the first few words of this flashback to see myself sitting on my bunk bed back in Abilene, Texas in a small room with blank, painted cement walls. The mind is such a complicated and at times a very terrible mechanism, and it can put you into a state of panic and leave you frozen in intense fear.

As I became older, I learned that our brains go through a process called 'hyper-encoding' when we are placed in traumatic situations. 'Hyper-encoding' is a process where we basically 'hard-code' a traumatic situation into our brains as fear kicks in that we are in a dangerous situation. As the memory sets itself into our brains it then separates itself into two diverse ways from a point of 'hyper-encoding' to 'minimal-encoding' which is how our brain protects us amid a traumatic event. We remember the beginning of the event as a means of protecting ourselves if we should ever find ourselves about to be placed in these situations again (hence hyper-encoding), but we may not remember the entire event or even remember the order in which things occurred within the event (minimal-encoding).

I first became aware of the terms, 'hyper-encoding' and 'minimal-encoding' while reading an article by Cara Kelly in *USA Today*, published on September 25, 2018. The article was speaking about the charges lobbied at the Supreme Court nominee Brett Kavanaugh by Dr. Christine Blasey Ford and another woman named Deborah Ramirez. Dr. Christine Blasey Ford stated that she was sexually assaulted by Supreme Court nominee Brett Kavanaugh when they were back in Yale sometime between 1983-1984. There were discussions held regarding the lapses in memory as recited by these women, centering on whether their memories could be perceived as accurate recollections since there were many gaps present. In the article, Jim Hopper, a Harvard Medical School consultant, and teaching associate is quoted as saying, "Just because there are pieces missing, doesn't mean those that remain aren't accurate, especially those central details of the experience that may be burned into the brain to the day they die."

The article continues, stating that "trauma can also enhance memories . . . the result of an evolutionary need for self-preservation. – As fear kicks in, the brain goes into a phase of hyper-encoding, or burning in, details about the beginnings of a dangerous scenario, such as the onset of sexual assault. It later shifts to a period of minimal encoding, when details not commanding the brain's attention aren't readily absorbed."

As an example, "an attack by a lion is more important in avoiding future attacks than whether the lion strikes with its right or left paw," hence the terms, 'hyper and minimal encoding are derived.

After hearing some of the recollections of my fellow veterans during our Military Sexual Trauma meetings at the VA hospital, I can tell you with certainty that claims of sexual assault in the military are still not being dealt with effectively. These veterans have all come away scarred, feeling as if they should not have said anything just so they could protect themselves and maintain their positions in the military.

Nurse Phyllis Simpson at the VA is my therapist, and together we worked through several different Post Traumatic Stress Disorder (PTSD) treatment modalities that have helped me learn more about my triggers and ways to help alleviate the symptoms brought about when I am experiencing an episode of PTSD. In addition to these modalities, I was also recommended to check out the Military Sexual Trauma (MST) Women's group led by Dr. Jessica McNeil. A referral was made for me for the group, and after about a week, I received a phone call from Dr. Jessica McNeil; we briefly discussed what the group was like, afterwards, she asked me if I would like to attend a session just to see how it feels. She stressed the fact that during the group sessions, we (military veterans and active-duty personnel) are not allowed to talk about our individual traumas (because we don't want to 'trigger' anyone in the group), but that the purpose of the group is for us to come together to talk about our lives and anything that's going on in our lives at the moment in an effort to help one another learn how to communicate and thrive in society. I told her that I liked the fact that we would not talk about our traumas and that I would like to attend a session and see how it felt.

I COUNT THE DARK

Dr. Jessica McNeil said 'Great, Tina, I'll put your name on the schedule, then, and you will receive a reminder in the mail telling you where to come. I said, "Ok." Thanked her and said, "I look forward to seeing you, then. Goodbye."

The day of the group meeting arrived, and I traveled down to the VA, parked my car, and went inside for the group meeting. Dr. McNeil started the meeting on time and the group consisted of about five other women besides me all sitting around in a semi-circle in a pretty big room at the VA on the 7th floor in the mental health wing of the building that's located in the South Wing of the hospital. I was a little nervous, so I did not make eye contact with any of the other women; I just stared at Dr. McNeil most of the time or stared down at the floor. I realized that I had dozed off there for a minute, and when I came back to the present, Dr. McNeil was saying, "These are the rules. First of all, whatever is said in the group, stays in the group, understood?"

Everyone either verbally stated OK or simply nodded their heads in agreement. "Next, we do not discuss individual traumas in the group because we don't want to trigger anyone else, and that's not the reason we are meeting here today. All of you have your own psychiatrists and therapists, and if there is anything said in group which you feel might trigger you, please just feel free to step outside of the room, gather yourself together, and when you can rejoin the group. If you feel that you cannot do that, then just let me know, and I will make sure that you get the treatment that you need. If you need to talk with your therapist or psychiatrist then we will handle that together – outside of this group. Understood?"

Again, everyone either verbally agreed or nodded their heads in agreement.

Dr. McNeil continued the group rules by explaining to everyone that we are here today to speak or if you feel more comfortable just being silent then you can be silent as well and just enjoy this time that we have together. Here is where you can talk about your day. Was there something that happened in your life today that you want to share with everyone? Is there anything going on in your family life that you want to share? I/we are here to see if we can help one another; see if I can help you learn how to handle life situations differently, possibly when you are triggered or even when you are not triggered. Literally, we can talk about anything here.

For example, how did it make you feel walking into the VA today? Did you feel comfortable? Uncomfortable? When you were on the elevator coming upstairs, how did you feel? Was there anything that happened on the elevator that made you feel uncomfortable or comfortable? Then Dr. McNeil went on to say that sometimes she has heard from other women that it can be a little uncomfortable getting off the elevator coming from the garage and having the door open out onto a sea of male faces, sometimes loud talking, sometimes maybe glancing up at you and it makes you feel uncomfortable. Her comment started the women to talk and one woman, let's call her Marcie, spoke up and mentioned how she doesn't like coming into the VA sometimes because there are always many men around, and it's not that any one of them does or says anything to her; it's just the fact that they are always grouped together, so, it makes her jumpy.

After Marcie said that another lady spoke up (let's call her Regina) and said she gets uncomfortable every time she is in an elevator with a group of men. It doesn't matter whether there are other women on the elevator or not, she will usually find herself getting off the elevator the very next time the door opens just so she can calm herself down. The conversation was really starting to pick up, and Dr. McNeil joined in and said that she realized this is a problem, so she talked it over with her colleagues. Together they came up with the idea to place posters all around the building asking veterans to be mindful of other veterans in the building when communicating in a loud manner and asking veterans to be respectful of one another. She stated that the campaign would be starting in the next month and asked all of us to let her know if we noticed a change in the atmosphere around the elevator lobby area and other places in the building, like the patient waiting rooms. We all said that we would agree to let her know.

At that time, Dr. McNeil let us all know that it was almost time to end the meeting. She realized that she did not allow everyone to officially greet one another at the start of the meeting, so she asked each one of us if we wouldn't mind just going around the room as we were about to close and stating our names, provided our branch of service, and say how we would like to be addressed while in the group, "...Mrs.... First name.... or just Last name, whatever you feel comfortable with, just let us know."

She started by stating her name and letting us know that we could call her Dr. McNeil, Dr. M, or Dr. Jessica McNeil.

As we went around the room, I learned that the majority of the women were former Active Duty Army, and most had separated from the military a while ago, just like me, but I was the only person there that day representing the United States Air Force. Group ended with Dr. McNeil giving us another reminder that what is said in the group stays in the group and letting everyone know that unless she receives a call or a message requesting that our names be canceled from the next meeting that she would send everyone a reminder for the next meeting.

I left the meeting feeling okay about attending because it seemed like it would be a nice, low-key, or no-pressure environment and provide me with the opportunity to meet some new people that are veterans like myself who might share some of the same goals of healing. The one bit of irony in the group for me though, is that it seems a little weird that we were all sitting in the Veterans Administration hospital building, being serviced by a licensed psychiatrist/therapist who represents the VA, and we are using the resources of the

VA, but No One from the VA will ever even acknowledge that something wrong was done to us or even apologize for the bad things that happened or are still happening to us in the military today.

The women veterans that I have met while attending the MST groups represent all branches of the military, all age ranges, and various ranks. Some of these ladies are just separating from the military after only serving one contract tour or after having been enlisted for many, many years. I remember the first time I met (let's call her Diane) at one of the meetings. Diane was about 26 years old, with brown eyes, black hair that was currently done up in a bun perched on the top of her head, and she was dressed in a pair of jeans, a black shirt buttoned up to the collar having just rushed to attend the meeting from her office which was located not too far from the VA hospital. Diane told us that she only enlisted because she wanted to get a college degree while also serving her country. She stated that she wasn't enlisted for more than two years before she was victimized and that when she reported her attack that she was instantly blackballed, which made making rank harder and harder for her after filing a complaint. She said that after that, she knew she couldn't stay in the military anymore, so when her time ended, she just decided to separate rather than stay in and get blocked for one reason or another trying to go further up the ladder for higher and higher ranks.

Diane is grateful that she has her benefits because she knew of friends of hers that didn't stay until the end of their contract and chose to separate early, and as a result, they did not receive the same type of benefits package that she did upon separation. For me, just hearing that there is a 'Diane story to tell' just filled me with anguish and anger that things are no better now than they were back in the late 1970s early 1980s for me and that doesn't even cover the experiences of the other women veterans who entered the military prior to 1979.

I COUNT THE DARK

Can we think about this for just a moment? The fact is that just from my experience alone, it is now 40 years later, and we are still no closer to resolving these types of crimes and injustices against women. How is that possible? We move four decades forward, and yet we are still behind the proverbial eight ball.

How is it possible for all of these different women, representing different ages, ethnic backgrounds, societal groups, etc., to have all had the same or similar experiences years and years apart with there still being no consistent and purposeful change in military policy to punish the perpetrators and not the victims? Every so often, there is an expose here or an article there that blows up in the media telling us something else shameful has been uncovered and that the military is doing its best to crack down on these occurrences, yet the same thing keeps occurring repeatedly.

We are in the midst of the #MeToo movement. We have lived through a period in time where there was a significant uptick in the reports of Domestic Violence/Spousal Abuse. Yet, still, there is no one longstanding period where justice appears to have been served so well that it became a strong deterrent towards these crimes ever happening again. Or, at the very least, there doesn't seem to be any indicators showing that potential perpetrators are so apprehensive and fearful of the system and what violating women would mean in terms of criminal charges against them that they think twice before becoming a perpetrator of one of these crimes.

People walk around every day with disabilities. Most of the time, we can easily identify a person with a disability because there is a visual, auditory, physical, or even mental disability that is most often noticeable, but for women that have been victims of sexual violence, we carry around a load of silent disabilities. Yesterday, today, and tomorrow we see that more and more women are in the trenches fighting a long and weary battle, and that battleground is the body of the woman herself.

My experience is likely not very different from that of other women who have been assaulted during their military service. I kept silent for more than 30 years and just tried to live my life. I carried the weight of shame with me for many reasons, but the most profound reason was that I did not feel that my experiences or feelings were valid, as I hadn't served during wartime and because I was a woman. I convinced myself that since I did not serve during wartime, I was not worthy of being given the title of Veteran of the United States Air Force. I convinced myself that since I did not serve in combat, my injuries were not as severe as any other military airman, so I had no reason to complain about anything.

I grew up thinking and believing that military veterans were soldiers like my brothers who had served in Vietnam and like my uncle, who served during the Korean war, or my father's brother and many other men in my family who had served in some type of conflict and were blessed enough to come home to their families and pick up their lives where they left off. I did not have any female examples of military veterans, so I suppose I also somehow thought that women who separated from the military were either called something else or simply not referred to at all. I know I never really gave it much thought at that time of my life.

My victimization in the Air Force during the late '70s and early '80s was not necessarily anything new; however, I do believe that the way my situation was handled or mishandled speaks directly to how women in the military were treated back then as well as how accusations of rape and sexual assault were viewed in society during that time. During that time, I do not recall hearing of any sexual assault cases that were investigated or prosecuted involving the military. In my specific case, I do not recall any legal action being taken, no joint interviews being held, or follow-up discussions of any kind. There were no big media exposes I can recall detailed in the newspaper during that time, and this was also pre-internet, FaceTime, Instagram, TikTok, etc. Accusations of sexual assault and abuse were handled in the most low-key and non-disruptive manner possible.

At the time of my attack, society did not seem to be as focused on a woman's behavior prior to an attack, or at least not to the degree where we picked apart every angle of rape from a woman's perspective when a rape occurred that was not sensationalized in the media. It was the rape of "Cheryl Ann Araujo in 1983" that led to 'victim blaming' and became the basis for the movie "The Accused" starring Jodie Foster. Then there were the sensationalized trials of both Mike Tyson in July 1991 and William Kennedy Smith in December 1991 that held aspects of victim-blaming as well, but again, things were different in 1979, 1980, and 1981 than they were in the early 1990s and vastly different from what we are experiencing now in the 21st century. Today we have the Federal Rape Shield law (circa 1994) in place, which helps protect women in most cases, but it took approximately 20 years for that to become a federal law from its early beginnings in 1974.

Early Life In North Philly

A sense of security is very important to me in life these days due to the traumatic events of the past. Sometimes the smallest things can provide a sense of warmth and security. The softness of a sweater can provoke a memory of being held in the gentleness of someone's arms, or the scent of a dryer sheet on my clothes can remind me of the aroma of burning incense as I meditate. Although times were not easy in the military, I continue to find solace in the little things, like methodically folding my clothes or tightening the corners of the bed so that when I slip into the sheets, all the fears of the night melt away because I have the sensation of being wrapped in a cocoon of warmth and security. There are some things that just never leave you, no matter how much time passes, even if you learned those routines decades ago.

I craved a sense of normalcy that was never present while growing up in North Philadelphia, as we were subject to random acts of violence from the gang wars and my first boyfriend, John Herman Oaks. One thing about the military that comforted me back then was how then I could rise and shine each morning and fall into bed every evening knowing exactly what was expected of me.

No one realizes how hard it is to be away from your entire family for the first time as a very young adult until you go through something like this yourself. While it is true that I chose this path, I still felt that it was forced on me because of my family situation. Growing up to be a strong, independent black woman was not an easy thing to do in North Philadelphia. Going to school in the 1970s meant having to contend with the violent gang wars and trying to steer clear of all the boys who just wanted to get in your pants and pop out baby after baby. I can still remember the time I was almost caught up during one of the gang wars between 'The Village' (Marston Street gang) and '2-9 D' (29th and Diamond street crew). Everybody on the block knew that the gang wars could happen at almost any time of the day or night, but most of the time, it seemed to coincide with school letting out between 3:00 pm and 4:00 pm so if you didn't want to get caught in-between you best be inside your house or somewhere else safe.

There was this one time when I stayed a little late after school to talk to my gym teacher Mrs. Smith, and I lost track of time. Normally, I would have either dance or gymnastics practice after school but on this day, practice was canceled, so I had a chance to talk with the teacher about some of the problems I was having with my floor routine and the horse (aka vault) so I took advantage of the time. Once we were finished talking, I started on my way home, and just as I was about halfway down my block walking towards my house I looked and saw groups of boys running towards me from both directions shouting and yelling. I looked around frantically for a place to hide and locked eyes with Mr. Ed Wilson, who lived across the street and just two doors down from my house. He yelled at me to, "Come and get inside this house now, girl!"

I ran across the street as fast as I could and just as he pulled me inside, I heard a scrape on the step and was grateful that he pulled me inside so quickly. Going on outside his door I could hear lots of shooting, smashing, thumping, and yelling and I could only imagine how badly someone was getting hurt at that moment. We moved quickly out of the living room into the dining room and Mr. Ed told me to get under the dining room table for the time being. It was always safer to hide somewhere and stay away from the windows because you could get shot by pellets from the bb guns or real bullets by standing too close to the windows.

During the gang wars, they used whatever they had to inflict harm: fists, sticks, stones, bats, knives, bb guns, and guns. Mr. Ed was on the phone talking with my mother telling her that I was alright and that he would keep me inside until all the fighting was over. I will never understand the territorial nature of those gang wars and no matter how many times my brothers tried to explain it to me it just never made sense to me that just because of a gang you couldn't walk down certain streets in the neighborhood or talk to certain people. A lot of people wound up disabled for life or dead because of the gang wars in the seventies. We had a funeral director who rode around with a casket on top of his hearse with a dummy in it symbolizing a dead person and he carried a bullhorn telling kids to stop killing each other. There was entirely too much senseless killing going on at the time and watching him drive around town was a good reminder of how important it was that people stop killing each other.

My brothers, James, Little Junior, and Jason were affected by the gang wars but not my eldest brother Jackson. Jackson enlisted when he was 16 and joined the United States Air Force and my brother James followed him in shortly afterward by joining the Marines instead. Although James enlisted and served during Vietnam like my brother Jackson, he couldn't truly escape the gang wars because on one fateful trip home after Vietnam he was assaulted by another gang member based on a beef they had long before he enlisted. This guy from another gang found out that my brother was home from Vietnam and decided to pay a visit when we were having a barbeque to celebrate my brother's return home. All I can recall is that they were playing cards on the steps while I was across the street at my best friend Angie's house who lived down the street from Mr. Ed. Suddenly, out of the corner of my eye, I saw my brother slumped over and the guy was running towards me next wielding a knife in his hand as if he wanted to stab me. Angie had just gone inside, and I was getting ready to go home but instead, I had to start running towards Mr. Ed's house, away from Angie's house, and once again Mr. Ed came to my rescue and pulled me inside his door as quick as possible before I wound up getting stabbed myself.

Although my brother survived the attack, he was left with more than 22 stitches from the tip of his collarbone all the way down to beneath his navel. Thinking back on that day, I don't know how Mr. Ed always wound up being my savior, but I'm so glad he did. He was a nice, kind older man with brown eyes and a light-skinned face. He always had a smile ready to greet you and help the kids on the block. I can remember also having a crush on his son, I think his name was Tony, but I'm not sure, either way, he was much older than me, so he was out of my league.

All the drama and danger that went on around me when I was growing up in North Philly is what convinced my Mom to help me sign up for the Air Force, a long-held secret dream of mine anyway. In her eyes, it was the safest thing for me to do so that I would not turn out to be just another young, unwed mother stuck in the ghetto with no way out or wind up getting hurt or killed.

After my near-death misses, I was very much on the path to becoming a young unwed mother, but Mama Ruth made sure she stopped that train right away. The memory of what happened back in ninth grade is still vivid; it has endured over my lifetime.

Years and years later, I would find myself thinking and wondering why Mama never explained her actions. I was fifteen, and I often wonder how much that time changed me forever. I believe my mother never spoke about the ordeal simply because she saw no reason to linger in the past. In her mind, I imagined, she had broken the Green family curse, so for her – problem solved. I never really knew what dreams my mother had for me because we really never spoke of them aloud, but I knew one thing for sure, and that was that I was never going to be stuck in North Philly, only having baby after baby, no future of a husband, with only two picture-perfect children and a warm, loving home to come home to daily.

She never wanted that life for my sisters either, but I think things or rather 'life' must have seemed more possible to her back when my sisters became pregnant but as time went on life became more of a struggle for my mom. She saw herself raising more grandchildren and maybe that prospect alone caused her to pay more attention to me and the life that I had been given.

Humphrey's Pills/Mama Ruth

BERTHIENNA EVELYN GREEN! Come here right now!"

What in the world had I done? Mama Ruth never called me by my full name unless I was in trouble. I was sitting upstairs in my room on my bed, just daydreaming as I stared at the blue wallpaper with twirling yellow tulips and light blue clouds. I was playing music in my room, just waiting for John, my boyfriend, to finish his homework and come take me out for a drive through Fairmount Park. I jumped up off my bed and ran to my mother's room to see what was wrong.

Mama looked at me and asked, "What is wrong with you? Are you crazy? How could you do this to me?"

"Mama, what is wrong?" I asked

Before I could say another word, Mama jumped up and slapped me clear across my face and I stumbled back onto her bed. Tears welled up in my eyes and I instantly started to cry. Mama had never smacked me before and just as quickly as I started to cry, Mama fell to her knees and just started crying and praying. I was still sitting on her bed and so I bent down to hug her and still crying I asked her, "What's wrong?"

"How could you do this to me? You are pregnant, silly chile! Go to your room and don't come out until I call you."

My mouth dropped open and I looked at Mama as if she was crazy because I would know if I was pregnant, I think? I didn't feel pregnant. I jumped up off Mama's bed and ran to my room, slamming the door as I fell onto my sister Shelley's bed. I almost hit my head on the top of the brown bunk bed with yellow comforters that I shared with my sister

Shelley. Shelley had the bottom bunk and I had the top bunk since I was the youngest, and she wanted to be the first one out of the room and into the bathroom every day. I came out of my daze and reached for the blue princess phone on the nightstand, picking it up so I could call John and see where he was. Mama was on the phone talking to grandmom Bertha about me being pregnant and how she was not going to let this happen again. I listened in on the phone, and Mama said that she was counting my pads and realized that I had not used any pads since last month, so she knew that I must have had sex and that I must be pregnant.

Grandma said, "Now, don't go jumping to any conclusions because you know this could all be a mistake. Maybe she was using some of Shelley's pads, and you just got confused."

Sighing and almost screaming into the phone, "No, mama, I counted Shelley's and Rita's pads, and their count is correct. The only count that's off is hers, so I know what I am talking about here."

Bertha asked, "Well, what are you going to do now?"

Ruth responded, "Well, didn't you tell me a long time ago that there is some sort of stuff that she could take that will make her period come on?"

Grandma answered, "Yeah baby, go get two bottles of Humphrey's pills from Mr. York's drugstore on 28th street and then go to the liquor store and get a bottle of Jacquin's Ginger Brandy and make her drink it straight down. By the time the pills are gone, she should have her period the next day. If you want to speed up the process, then just get two bottles of Brandy and that should make her period come on even faster with her taking the pills."

Mama, heaving a sigh of relief somewhat, said, "Ok mama, thanks. I'll talk to you later."

Mama and grandmom hung up the phone and then I hung up the extension softly, so Mama would not know I was listening in.

Don't ask me why but I just started crying out of nowhere after hearing everything that I just heard. I was crying because I was pregnant; my mother knew I was pregnant before I did; John and I were going to be parents; Mama wanted me not to be pregnant, and now I was supposed to take some pills and alcohol to kill my baby! As quickly as I started crying, I had to stop and call John real fast to tell him not to come over because all hell would surely break loose if he showed up at my door right now. I reached for the extension, being careful to pick up the phone softly, and heard the dial tone. Thankfully no one was on the phone.

"John, hey babe, I can't go for a ride tonight. Can we get together tomorrow, baby?"

John answered me, "Sure, baby. I have to work on my dad's car tonight anyway, so I was just about to call you and cancel tonight."

"Oh, okay. Work on your dad's car, and I'll talk to you tomorrow. Smooches, sweetie."

John said goodnight, and we hung up the phone. I was so glad that we didn't talk long because I didn't want mama to pick up the phone again. I didn't tell John anything about being pregnant. I wanted to wait until I had a chance to really understand everything that was happening to me first.

I was still having a hard time digesting what I heard Mama say on the phone to grandmom, "She's not going to have to turn out like Rita and Shelley by becoming a teenage mother."

So, she made sure that she kept track of how many maxi pads we all used monthly. Who does that? Counts maxi pads monthly. Ruthie Mae that's who – a mother who has three daughters, two of which had babies at 15 years of age. She was determined to break the 'curse,' as she saw it, with me. Mama's purpose was for me to graduate high school without birthing a child out of wedlock and then go on and lead a successful life. Having a baby at 15 would have killed her dream for me so there was no other option in her mind other than to find a way to get rid of the baby quickly.

My experience was so surreal from the moment I looked into my mother's eyes and saw how disappointed she was in me that I somehow had sex without her knowing it and then became pregnant. Mama set up an appointment for me to go to the doctor for a pregnancy test the next day. I remember when we got home from the doctor's office and how frantically she began searching my room for traces of John being there. I don't know what she thought she would find, but when she found a condom, she began screaming at me, "If you had it, then why didn't you use it? Stupid, just stupid, and dumb, Dammit! This is not happening again! Just because your sisters had babies at 15 doesn't mean you are going to follow right behind them and do the same thing. Not today. Somebody is going to make something out of themselves between one of you, and since you are my last daughter, well, then it has to be you. Go to your room, and don't come out until I call for you."

I sat on the bed shaking, crying, befuddled, not knowing what to say in my defense. Now that I look back on that time, it does seem pretty stupid and dumb for John to have given me a condom, and yet we chose not to use it. I don't remember why we didn't use it or even if we spoke about using it at all. Either way, it didn't matter one bit to my mom because she was livid! She made me stay in my room until she called for me to come downstairs.

I did as I was told and was surprised to be awakened by my sister Rita and told to come downstairs. I was so emotionally exhausted that I fell asleep waiting for mama to call me downstairs. When I got downstairs Rita told me to sit down. Shelley poured me a glass of Ginger brandy and gave me a handful of pills saying 'Drink this down and take these pills. Me: What? What are you talking about? Mama was sitting on the green couch in the living room watching tv, so I started to get up from the table and go talk to her. Rita frowned, her face up, and said, "Sit down, child! My sister had a way of saying the word 'child' in such a patronizing tone that made me angry all the time. It's as if she thought I was no better than a bug on her shoe that she was trying to smash. She turned towards my sister and told her to "give me the glass and those pills again. Mama said you are going to drink this brandy and swallow all these pills before night comes."

I looked into Shelley's eyes and saw tears welling up in her eyes and knew she didn't want to do it, but she turned towards me and handed me the glass and the pills. I have never had alcohol in my life before, so I didn't know what to expect. I put a handful of the pills in my mouth and reached for the brandy. I gagged before I could even get the glass to my mouth because the smell of the brandy was overpowering. Suddenly, I felt the tears fall on my face, and my sister Shelley lifted my hand again and brought the glass to my lips, forcing me to swallow some of the brandy and swallow the pills.

Rita stood facing me with the meanest look on her face, saying, "We are all going to sit here all night if we have to until you finish all of these pills and the Brandy."

To this day, I still cannot really fathom the reality of being pregnant so young and having an abortion. That entire experience seems like something out of a dream because of how my mother handled the situation. I detached myself from the entire experience and went through my ninth-grade year of school like a walking zombie, dazed, confused, and barely functioning.

In 1975, no one in my family was saying words like 'have a miscarriage,' or 'fetuses,' or 'dead baby,' or anything close to the reality of what my mom wanted to happen but she learned from my grandmother that if you wanted to force your period to come on that you must take these 'Humphrey's pills and drink alcohol so she figured she would try it with me.

Somehow, I made it thru half a bottle of brandy and almost one whole bottle of Humphrey's pills before I started to feel this weird feeling in my stomach. My mouth started to water, and I was having trouble sitting up straight. I tried to speak, and the words wouldn't come out of my mouth. Rita looked at me weirdly and started to say something, but before she could get the words out of her mouth, I sprang up out of my chair, leaned into her, and threw up in her lap. She started patting my back hard, and my eyes were watering, and sweat was pouring off my head like crazy.

Rita looked at my sister and said, "Quick, go get the trash can from the kitchen."

Shelley ran to the kitchen and got the trash can for me to vomit in just in the nick of time because Rita turned my head sideways, and then it happened again. Now I was crying full out and vomiting at the same time. Rita had left to go change her clothes, and Shelley got the dishrag from out of the kitchen and wiped my face. There were no paper towels in the kitchen, so Shelley grabbed one of the kitchen towels and used that to wipe my blouse off, and helped me to sit up straight in my chair. I was able to put my lips together to ask for some water to clean my mouth out and Shelley got up and got me a glass of water.

Shelley said, "Don't drink the water just use it to rinse your mouth out or you will throw up again."

I put the water in my mouth and then spit the rest into that nasty trash can. I almost threw up again when I leaned over to spit in the trash can because it smelled horrible. I could see pieces of the bologna sandwich and the apple I had for lunch all mixed in the trash can. Yuck. The smell of the brandy seemed ten times stronger in the trash can than it did on my blouse.

Mama Ruth stared at me for what seemed like a long time and finally said, "Are you alright?" I couldn't even get words out of my mouth because I started to cry again. Mama turned around, picked up her newspaper, and started to do her crossword puzzle again, paying me no mind. My eyes shifted to the china cabinet and landed on the picture of John F Kennedy and Martin Luther King, Jr. that Grandmom gave to mama to display in the china cabinet. All black families had the same picture hanging up in their house of Dr. Martin Luther King, Jr, and John F. Kennedy. Back in the day, those two men were revered by the black race. Personally, I saw Dr. King as a savior and a friend to every black person in America for all that he did on our behalf.

I sat there staring at those pictures, wondering what Martin Luther King, Jr would say to my mama if he were here now. Wondering what my father would say if he knew mama was making me drink this horrible stuff, take pills, get drunk and throw up all over the place. I'll never know because it's not as if mama and daddy talk all the time since he's married to another woman living way down near 19th and Lehigh Streets.

Is this cruel and unusual punishment? Yes, in my book, it most certainly did fit the bill of cruel and unusual punishment.

Rita came back into the dining room and poured me another hefty glass of brandy and opened the second bottle of Humphrey's pills and says, "Drink it slower this time instead of as fast as you were doing earlier, and you won't throw up so fast dummy."

I looked at Rita and, at that moment, I wanted to smack the stuffing out of her, but I knew she would beat me to a pulp because my sister had the heaviest hands of anyone that I knew. When she hits you, it's like a brick upside your head.

I started drinking again and noticed when I turned to look in the living room that my mother was nowhere to be found. The tv was still on and the Jefferson's was starting to come on. In my head, the theme song that was playing was a joke because I was not "moving on up" as they sang on the tv. I was sinking down, down, down into that awful bottle of Ginger Brandy. Mama Ruth must have slipped out and gone upstairs just after Rita came down. All I can remember about that night is getting so sick of the ginger brandy, vomiting multiple times, and pleading with my sisters to stop but all of this was to no avail because they were told to do this, and they weren't going to stop until my mother told them it was ok.

At some point during the night, my sisters took pity on me and put me to bed but not before I had finished all the pills and I think a bottle and a half of that nasty ginger brandy. The end of this sad tale is that none of the pills nor the brandy worked so my mother was forced to try to figure out how I was going to get an abortion in 1975. This was still somewhat hard to do in 1975 for a family on welfare and only two years after abortions had become legal in the United States. I don't know what she went through to get the procedure done, but I know that there was never a question in her mind that I would have an abortion because she was on a mission to make sure that I did not have a child at 15 like my other sisters. I think that must have been all she thought about as I was growing up.

I remember being taken to the doctor's office for the procedure but for some reason, I cannot remember the actual procedure itself. I believe, in some ways, my brain decided to pull me away from the experience because of how painful it was so that I could continue to function as a human being. I am stunned into silence every single time I sit back reflecting on the path my life's journey has taken me on since the early days of living in North Philly.

I continue to be amazed at the tenacity that I have for life, my life and that of those whom I love and share this space with today. My life is a living testimony to perseverance bearing witness to more than 40 years of abuse and suffering. There are many medical professionals today reporting on the certainty of correlations between abuse, suffering and their impact on mental illness. All we need do is reflect back on the times that we find ourselves living in today to see the amplification of their reports in real time. Acknowledging those perspectives, I now believe that it is possible that my earlier experiences as a teenager growing up in North Philadelphia somehow primed me to be victimized in the USAF.

So, I had an abortion at the age of 15 and experienced my first episode of drunkenness, albeit 'controlled,' it was still a horrible experience to go through as a 15-year-old girl. At the age of 15, I know for a fact that I never had the chance to even consider what being 15 and pregnant was all about, much less being pregnant one moment and not pregnant the next. I never had the chance to be happy at the thought of bringing a new life into this world because I never even knew I was pregnant until my mother took me to the doctor. Years later, mama told me that when she went to count my maxi-pads that time in 1975 that she realized I must not have used any that month, so she figured something was awry but never expected in a million years that I, her youngest and most accomplished daughter would be pregnant. That was the only mention of the entire incident, and to this day, I cannot even recall how that tidbit found its way into a conversation we were having or what the conversation was even about because we never discussed pregnancies in much detail even when I became pregnant later in life.

I also never really experienced the loss that comes along with abortion because I closed my mind off to the experience. Who might that child have become? Would John and I have gotten married? How different might my life have been if I had been allowed to go down that path?

This was only one of the many traumatic events I have suffered through in my life. I learned much later in life that the notion of using Humphrey's pills and a bottle of gin was nothing but an old wives' tale because it did nothing to cause abortions or bring about the onset of menstruation. I suppose it never dawned on my mom or sisters at that time that I could have also died of alcohol poisoning due to being forced to drink such a large quantity of alcohol all at once. It really boggles my mind to think of all the terrible things that could have happened to me that night. It also astounds me that my mother could maintain such a singular focus on ensuring that I would no longer be pregnant that this thought consumed her causing all rational thoughts to be totally eradicated from her mind. Reckless, to say the least, not to mention the everlasting effect it had on my life.

My mother must have had some sort of wonderful, fabulous plan for my life, but she never shared it with me. As a preteen, she made certain that I went to summer camps outside of the city with white kids. One summer, I remembered that my brother Jason and I spent part of the summer with a white family, learning how to fish and seeing how the better half lived. I believed my mother wanted desperately to expose me to life outside of North Philadelphia. I also believed that she wanted to expose me to the arts, so she enrolled me in Freedom Theatre. Everything that she did for me was meant to shape me into a person who had choices and options in life outside of sex, drugs, and pregnancies that other girls were having, my sisters, included, in North Philadelphia

I know I am a much different person because of having gone through those experiences, but what I don't know and will never know is who I might have become if I had carried that child to term and delivered a healthy baby. I imagined the events of 1980 would never have happened and that I would have made a career in the military. The path that befell my sisters altered their lives, that much I know, my eldest sister, Rita, had a child at age 16 and Shelley had a child at age 15. Mama Ruth was totally against me having a child in my teens as well. One thing that I did not know then was that the experiences to come would somehow, no matter how devastating they were, shape me into the strong-willed,

I COUNT THE DARK

intelligent, forward thinker that I am today. Out of adversity comes strength and resolve.

WSJ Article And My First Attempt To File

I came across an article online that was published by the Washington Post on June 28, 2012 (my birthday, I might add), which chronicled a sexual abuse scandal purportedly held at Lackland AFB, San Antonia, Texas. The article spoke about a number of training instructors at Lackland AFB who were being charged with sexual abuse of training recruits. Although my abuse did not happen at Lackland AFB the article just brought to light the fact that 33 years later, airmen were still being assaulted and raped under the command of their superior officers and training instructors.

Shortly after that story came out, I started becoming aware that there were other stories being published about sexual abuse in the military. As these stories started to become more and more widespread, I started experiencing flashbacks to my attacks in the military. (Armor splitting wide open now). I spoke with one of my friends about what I was feeling, and he convinced me to file a claim with the Department of Veterans Affairs explaining my experience in the military.

I had never considered, nor was I even aware, that I could file a claim with Veterans Affairs chronicling my experience in the military. I had no idea what 'filing a claim' would do for me. I had only recently come to terms with my rape and sexual assault and decided that I needed to take some type of action to heal myself. After many days and nights, I had decided that I wanted an apology from the Air

Force. In retrospect, I realize how naïve and silly I was being to expect a huge institution like the United States Air Force to issue a formal apology to me, a silly little black girl from North Philadelphia, PA. No matter how silly it seemed it is all I ever really wanted – I wanted someone to be accountable for what happened to me that changed the course of my life forever. All I ever dreamed of growing up as a little girl was starry-eyed visions of flying around in airplanes in the military, jetting off to beautiful places, and living the life of an air force sergeant or some other lofty rank. The idea of being a strong, black woman in charge of other recruits in the military was appealing to me at 9 years of age but my dream was stomped on and never became a reality. So, after thinking long and hard about the suggestion from my friend, I decided to go ahead and apply to the VA and see what would happen from there. I put my dreams aside for the time being and thrust myself head-first into the application process.

I sat down one Saturday afternoon in May of 2012 with the intention of recalling my experience and submitting my application for disability. I had barely typed five words when I felt the warm water sliding down my face and realized that I was crying silently as my vision became cloudy due to my tears. I started wiping the tears away and managed to type a few more words before stopping as my body started shaking, and I began to cry more uncontrollably. Turning off my computer and sitting silently for almost an hour, I was finally able to compose myself. This was my cue that it was too soon to attempt to write anything down.

It would be two more years before I could bring myself to approach this task again, before I could muster the strength to face the many violations and assaults I experienced in the military before I could begin the process that would bring me home to myself, to claim my right to be believed, to be heard, and to be safe as a girl child and a woman.

John Herman Oaks (Deceased), and me on his junior prom at Benjamin Franklin High School.

I COUNT THE DARK

James Wilson Green, Brother (Deceased)

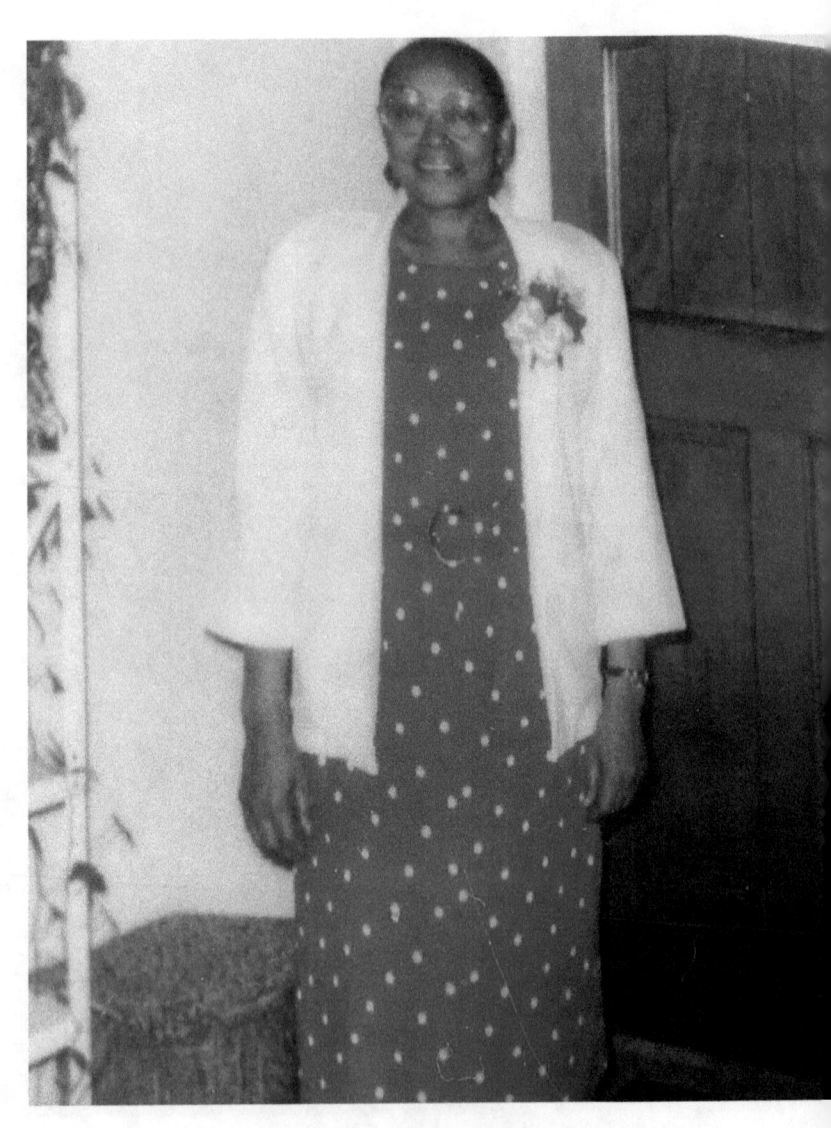

BERTHIENNA E. GREEN

Ruthiemae Ford, Mother (Deceased)

Shelley, BerthaMae Ford, (Deceased) RuthieMae Ford, (Deceased)

Rodney and Tiffany

I COUNT THE DARK

Airman Green, USAF

BERTHIENNA E. GREEN

Airman Green, B E

Good Luck Cake, Freedom Theatre, 1979

Jeffrey D. Russell Aka Davis And Me

I COUNT THE DARK

Ruthiemae Ford-Green-Reed in her heyday.

My AF Bestie, Myra Ratchford-Neely

Goodbye Philly, Hello USAF

Marvin Gaye's "I Heard It Through the Grapevine" swirled around us as we swayed on the dance floor. I was in the middle of the bodies, and I threw my head back, smiling and laughing along with my family and friends. It was late September 1979 and this was my going-away party, in the basement of Freedom Theatre at Broad and Master streets in Philadelphia. My whole family except my brother Jackson was there. My brother James and my sister Shelley were dancing together. James was wearing another of his designer creations, a denim jacket with a green, black, orange, and blue multi-colored silk shirt over a pair of denim bell-bottoms. My brother looked so good with his perfect medium cocoa-chocolate brown skin tone and his pencil-thin mustache. As usual, he was sticking out his tongue as he danced up a storm. Shelley was wearing a tan-colored jumper, her neatly coiffed, Afro-shining glory, all over her light-skinned self. Both were sweating out there.

Over in the corner, I spied my brothers Jason and Little Junior talking to some friends and my sister Rita was talking with my Mom, Ruthie Mae, over near the dessert table. My eldest brother, Joseph Jackson Abel, was in the Air Force stationed in the Philippines and was unable to get home to attend the party. Jason was dressed in a black shirt and blue jeans and I could tell from the way he was leaning into my friend, Mabel, that he was trying to "mack" on her right there. But Mabel wasn't having any of it: she pulled her body away from him and scanned the room to lock eyes with me, giving me the message that my brother better back up off her. I started laughing and shrugged my shoulders when she looked my way as if the tell her "you got this girl, handle him." My brother Little Junior, in his checkered shirt and black pants, wasn't doing much better in the way of "macking" as he tried to chat up Samantha, or Sam as we called here, over near the punch table. Samantha didn't look my way but she didn't have to because I could tell by how she got up and moved away from my brother that she knew how to handle her business.

My sister, Rita was dressed in a black, yellow, and white midi dress; her white boots made her seem taller than her 5.6-inch frame. She was talking to Mama but from this distance, I couldn't make out what they were saying, though I figured it must have had something to do with the macaroni and tuna salad because my sister was gesturing towards the bowl as she picked it up and took it back to the kitchen. Mama Ruth was dressed spectacularly as usual in her black and white wraparound dress with a black turban; with her light-mocha chocolate complexion and her perfectly sculpted eyebrows, she looked like a queen. Mama Ruth lost her eyebrows at 15 and had penciled them in ever since; I've never seen her eyebrows messed up – *ever*. She was a master at applying makeup; though she never wore foundation, her eyes and lips were always perfect. I just loved me some Mama Ruth.

Eventually, everyone was on the floor dancing and shouting at the top of their lungs. My boyfriend Davis (aka Jeffrey D Russell) worked the turntables and chose the perfect mix of rhythm and blues, soul, reggae, and pop music from the late Seventies. He was a master mix-master, and everyone jammed to his beats all night long. Davis was a light-skinned black man with muscles in all the right places from his chest all the way down to that perfectly shaped rear end. I loved me some of that man. His lips were perfect and he had the deepest brown eyes I'd ever seen on a black man, which is why every time he looked at me, I just melted and became instantly wet. Davis had on a white t-shirt with the sleeves rolled all the way to the top of his armpits and I could see his thigh muscles bulging out of those jeans. I couldn't wait to pull his pants off of him later that night.

"Hey everybody, it's time to cut the cake," Mama shouted, telling Davis to "cut that music down, please?" Davis turned the music down low and came to stand beside me at the head of the table. (I stood there smiling and grinning from ear to ear as if I had just won the biggest prize in the world. I felt so glad to be standing here in front of my family and my best friends from Freedom Theater and Murrell Dobbins Area Vocational Technical High School graduating class of 1978; "Moving in the Key of Life" was our motto that year).

Mama came around to the front of the table with me and Davis and everyone quieted down to hear her speak, "To my dearest daughter, Berthienna Evelyn Green, I am sorry to see you go but I do wish you much success in the United States Airforce. I can't believe you are all grown up now and about to fly off to Texas, of all places, and be miles and miles away from me."

She started to tear up now and gave me a great big hug, squeezing me so tight that I started to cry a little as well. After just a minute Mama straightened up and turned to the crowd and said… "Everyone please continue to pray for her while she is away from us and give her lots of hugs and kisses tonight."

She then turned to Davis, "Davis, I don't know what you are gonna do without her but I'm sure you'll be making lots of trips to Texas while she's away."

She then turned back to me. "Congratulations on joining the United States Airforce! Love you, sweetie."

Mama planted a big kiss on my forehead and then raised the knife to cut the cake.

Davis and I turned from the table and he pulled me inside the DJ booth and told me how much he loved me and how proud he was of me. Tears formed in his eyes as we began to kiss. Davis and I cuddled in the booth for a few moments longer and suddenly Mama was at the booth saying, "Come on out here and get some hugs from other people."

I started walking back to the cake table and people were grabbing at me as I walked by, pulling me into one big hug after the next. I teared up when Mama Sue hugged me and Kenneth D. Jones, Jr., Ms. Renee and Barry Henson, Jr., and all my other Freedom Theatre family members gave me hugs as well.

Tiffany Snyder and Rodney approached and we started talking about me signing up for the military. Tiffany stared me down in that way she had that always made me feel as if I was lost or something, saying: "I still cannot believe that you're really doing this."

I raised my hands, exasperated, "I'm really doing this, and there's no turning back now. I know I could stay in Philly and keep dancing and acting in plays and stuff, trying to make a life for myself in theatre, but that won't change what's going on at home and around my neighborhood. You know the gang wars have become just too unpredictable and dangerous. I also have to contend with all the young boys in the neighborhood trying their best to get in my pants even though I'm dating Davis."

She shook her head and frowned. "You're just going to be wasting all your talent by going into the Air Force. What in the world are you going to be doing in there? Do they even have a place for you to sing and dance?"

She crossed her arms, and I knew that no matter what I said that there was no convincing her. "The recruiter told me that they have a band and the USO, so I could try out for that if I really wanted to get some theatre in while I'm away."

I pulled her in for a hug. "I know it's going to be hard, but I feel like I'm ready."

She held on, hugging me back, and then pulled away. I noticed the first tiny little tear begin to drop. "What about you and Davis?" she asked.

I grinned, trying to cheer her up. "We'll still be together. He'll come down to Texas as soon as he can, but in the interim, we'll write to each other. As soon as I get permission for phone calls we'll have that as well. It's going to be hard, but I also believe it's going to be alright. I've gotta get out of here because I can't take it anymore. I feel like if I stay I'll just end up being another girl from North Philly that doesn't go anywhere and winds up having baby after baby, and that's all my life will be about."

I stopped and looked across the room at Mama Ruth. "At least as far as Mama's concerned, that's all my life in Philly would have been about—taking care of kids and no husband. And I don't want Davis to feel like he's stuck with me and that maybe I forced him to be with me just to have babies." I turned back to Tiffany and sighed. "Look, you know how close I came to taking that full scholarship to Wilberforce and majoring in journalism, but I can't even think about that now."

Tiffany nodded, and the slightest smile began to cross her face.

"Look, it's not like Davis and I are ready to start living together right now. He's still living with his grandmother and I can't ask him to leave her just to be with me. Honestly, I knew he would have done it but I didn't want him to have to make a choice that he might one day come to regret."

Tiffany and Rodney looked at me intently and I could tell they were finally in agreement even if they didn't say the words out loud. I saw them glance at each other and I knew I was finally in the clear. Tiffany pulled me in for another big hug. "Things won't be the same without you around, you do know that don't you? Now, who am I going to work out with every day practicing our dance moves after school?

Who's going to get up early every Saturday and head down here to catch an extra Creative dance class before rehearsals?

I laughed. "You'll just naturally start hanging out more with Paula, Cyndy, and Mabel."

Rodney smirked and tried hard to pull himself together before laughing out loud but Tiffany pouted. I pulled them both into a big bear hug. "You guys just hang onto each other and that will give me hope that Davis and I will be alright." I turned my head away as I teared up, thinking about being miles away from them and especially Davis. I shook my head at the thought of also being miles and miles away from Mama and my siblings as well. I turned back towards them both.

"You'd better write back when I write you... I mean it! Finally, we all hugged, and Rodney broke away first.

"Alright, alright, y'all need to stop talking so much. Let's go get some more food. I'm starving."

Then Davis and I were in the middle of the dance floor just dancing up a storm to a fast beat, and then Davis went back to the DJ booth to play one of our favorite slow songs, "Quiet Storm" by Smokey Robinson. We started grinding as we talked about Texas and when he could come down to see me.

Davis planted the tiniest and sweetest kisses on my left ear lobe. "I've been thinking about driving down to Texas in January right after you finish all your basic training, and maybe we can see each other then."

I pulled him even closer, nestling my neck up towards his lips. "That sounds good, but I don't know what's going to happen after I finish training, babe. Maybe we should hold off on making any plans for the moment." I began to realize that I had no idea whether I'd be staying in the same location or if I would be shipped off somewhere else right after Basic. "I promise, sweetie, to write as soon as I get the chance, and as soon as I know something specific about my destination, you'll be the first to know." "You Know How to Love Me

I COUNT THE DARK

and Make Me Feel So Good" by Harold Melvin and the Blue Notes came on and I leaned into his ear.

"Baby, I'm going to miss you soooooo much. I don't even know how to think when I'm away from you."

He pulled me in tighter, and my face brushed up against his Radio 437 t-shirt. I lay my head on his chest and breathed in his scent – Jovan musk blending nicely with his sweat. "I feel like I miss you already and you haven't even left yet. "Damn, Bubblegum," he said, using his nickname for me because he says I'm as sweet as double-bubble bubblegum. "What am I going to do without you? I'm so proud of you, baby, but I still wish there was a way for us to get out of Philly together and live somewhere so that you didn't feel like you had to leave."

I sighed as a few tears fell and Davis kissed them away as he told me he knew things were not great at home, but that this was going to be so hard on both of us. We kept dancing and listened intently to every word he said. Finally, the song ended and we left the dance floor just holding each other and thinking about what was to come….

Early the next morning Mama Ruth took me down to Broad Street to the recruitment office where I got sworn in and boarded the bus to San Antonio, Texas. I walked in wearing blue jeans and a button-down plaid shirt with stripes of blue and yellow against a red background. Mama wore black slacks, a white top, and gold hoop earrings. The recruiter told me to stand up and lift my right hand, palm facing forward as he recited the pledge. I repeated after him. "I, Berthienna Evelyn Green …"

Daydreaming 101

As the recruiter was speaking, I heard myself repeating every word and as every word crossed my lips, memory after memory came flooding into view. I saw myself standing on my friend Angie's steps chewing a big wad of bubble gum while listening to her tell me about the last time her and her boyfriend had gone to the movies. Then that image floated away and I remember hanging onto Angie's railing from the top marble step, jumping down quickly because Mama Ruth was calling me to come home.

Unbeknownst to me at the time, when I jumped down my left leg landed in Angie's trash can where there was a big shard of glass protruding that somehow sliced into my left calf but I never even felt it happen. As I was running home, I do recall feeling something warm running down my leg but paid it no mind because I had to get home pdq (pretty darn quick, as we used to say back in the day) when Momma called. I remembered hearing Angie screaming my name and yelling at the top of her lungs trying to get my attention but I was running fast to get home so I didn't turn back to see why she was screaming at all. No sooner than I landed at my front door, Momma who was watching me as I was running toward her, was screaming at the top of her lungs. I was totally confused as to why she was screaming because I couldn't imagine what I had done that was so wrong. Then the image shifted yet again and I was lying in the front seat of my dad's Cadillac with Mama holding a tightly wound towel around my left calf to stop the blood from escaping all over the place. My daddy drove that Cadillac like a 'bat outta hell' to get me to the hospital in a rush where I received 13 stitches in my left calf as a result of the cut to my leg.

I remember how much everyone was worried about me as they wondered what happened and why I needed to be rushed to the hospital. Angie's mom, the always sweet and wonderful, Mrs. Ruby Wise was so upset and hurt that I was hurt that she came over the house to make sure that I was ok. Momma made sure to call back home to let everyone on the block know that I was ok after all. The way I was raised back in the day was all about being raised by 'a village' and everyone on the 2400 block of Marston street was a part of my village. If one momma's child got hurt, it was like everyone's child got hurt and the entire block turned out in full force to make sure you healed well, they made sure you had the best eats to heal from as well. I remember how scared and upset Angie was and I couldn't wait to see her again just to let her and her mom, Mrs. Ruby know that everything was ok and no need to worry about me anymore. Back in the day, peeps were not into all the yelling and fussing and blaming like they are today because when one of us got hurt, we all felt it as if it happened to one of our own. To this day, I still do not recall why Momma called my name in the first place, minimal encoding at work again.

I was thinking about so many things as I took my oath. My life was about to change drastically, and I felt the need to wrap every experience up into a tight little box so that I could keep it close by, ready to whip it out whenever I felt really lonely way down there in Texas. I drifted back to the present when I realized that my swearing in had come to an end. I raised my shoulders up just a bit at the end to bring myself back to the present.

Duty Begins...

Once I was sworn in, I was given a few minutes to say goodbye to Mama. She drew me in with her smile and pulled me to her chest where I got a strong whiff of her Jergens lotion mixed with Jean Nate After Bath Splash. "Be strong, write often, pay attention in class, and make me proud."

I lifted my tear-stained face to look into her beautiful brown eyes. "I'll be strong, and I will write as often as I can. Mama, please take care of yourself. Oh, and I folded up a lot of tissues this morning, a whole box before you woke up, so you'll have enough to last for a while."

This was our nightly routine. When she would go out to work at the bar in the evening, I would fold up tissues for her to take with her because she had a habit of sweating from her eyes and over her top lip—she used the tissues to blot away the sweat. I knew Mama would be fine while I was away because my sister Shelley would step up and take my place.

It was a very hard, tearful goodbye, and I cried so hard I could barely see. The recruiter was very nice; he offered me a tissue and sent my mother off with a stern handshake. "Airman Green will be okay, ma'am. Everything will be alright." He turned to me and gave me the order to pick up my bag and head outside to the bus. I knew how serious my decision was from this point forward. All the paperwork up until this moment was just me signing my name on the dotted line, but it wasn't real then, but now it was. I boarded the bus when my name was called and sat down next to a stranger. We both looked at each other nervously. I felt a tinge of fear because I had no idea what would happen next, but I knew there was no turning back now. From that moment forward my life was about to change forever, either for good or for bad, but hopefully for the better.

Basic Military Training Squadron (BMTS), Lackland, AFB

"GET UP! GET UP! WHAT ARE YOU DOING SLEEPING? DIDN'T YOU GET ENOUGH SLEEP AT HOME! GET YOUR ASSES UP AND GET OFF THIS BUS NOW!"

As I jumped up out of my seat my head hit the metal rack above me. All I could see in front of me were two people dressed in military uniforms yelling at other people to get off the bus. It was the middle of the night somewhere in Texas and the lights were now on as a voice continued to yell in my ear. Everybody was scrambling about tripping over each other to get off the bus. I joined the group of confused teenagers and ran off the bus. All the yelling just sounded like a bunch of mixed-up words. I couldn't even make out the rest of it. All I knew was that I had to get off that bus right away.

Amid the confusion, we were told to line up and stand straight and tall. The dust we kicked up getting off the bus made several of us sneeze (me included) and cough like we've never seen dust in the dark of our basements ever before, but this was nothing like the dust kicked up in a basement. The bus was parked in what looked like a big flat field. we kicked up dust along the gravel road as we shuffled about to line up shoulder-to-shoulder on the berm. It was still dark so I knew we had been riding for hours.

The rest of the night transpired in a whirl of motion with more yelling and screaming as we were moved to processing, picked up paperwork, and got a haircut—girls and boys alike and it was a butch haircut if ever I'd seen one. I had no idea how I was going to style my hair after that cut. We were then directed to medical processing for our physical, hearing, and vision tests, glasses were issued as necessary (the frames were regulation and unflattering) and we received even more paperwork. Next, we were issued a uniform and then we made our first trip to the Base Exchange to pick up other necessary items like caps, shoe polish, etc. More paperwork was distributed as we were made to disrobe and get into our issued uniforms while being yelled at for being too slow— "Move! Move! Move!"—and then more paperwork slammed on top of the already burgeoning file perched precariously in our outstretched arms but somehow, we all knew you'd better not drop a thing because it would only be followed by more yelling. Finally, we were marched to our barracks and made to stand outside with our arms outstretched holding our clothes and lots of papers as we were subjected to more yelling.

Throughout all the yelling I was made to understand that I was now the property of the United States Airforce, and I wasn't to move without being told where to go and how fast to get there. I was informed that this was where my training would begin, and I'd remain there for the next 6 weeks. I am also told who my base commander is, who my direct command Sergeant is, and who my Technical Instructor (T. I.) is (SSgt. C. Brandert). We were informed that someone may be chosen for squad leader of squad # 3743 and that that squad leader would get to wear a green belt on their arm to show they're in command of the squad under the direction of the T. I. I made up my mind right then and there that I would be a squad leader.

After I don't know how many hours of moving and yelling and moving and yelling again, we reached our barracks and were told to run upstairs, find our bunk (identified by your last name and the last four of your social security number), and stand in front of it until given our next order. The grey metal bunks were lined up alongside both walls parallel to one another. All the beds were made up of white sheets and covered with dark green blankets. Those beds did not look comfortable at all. I could not imagine that I would ever get a good night's sleep on a metal cot that was supposed to be a bed. The T. I., Staff Sergeant Brandert (first name Christine), and her second in command Sgt Lopez were the only two people we were to listen to; they would accompany those of us who made it through the 6 weeks of Basic Training at Lackland Airforce Base, "Gateway to the Air Force," in San Antonio, Texas.

Staff Sergeant Brandert started yelling at us all over again as she showed us a short grey footlocker and a tall grey storage locker (a little over 5 feet) and explained how our clothes were supposed to be placed in both lockers.

"Drill inspections at 0530 hours every morning. Beds! Lockers! Boots!"

I waited for someone to show us how to spit-shine those boots but that didn't happen right then. Once again, I realized I had gone into another daze. I reminded myself to pay close attention and to stop being so spacey.

Next Staff Sergeant Brandert opened the tall standing locker to demonstrate how to hang our uniforms inside so that the shoulders of each uniform show the crease and are all facing forward in the same direction. Twenty-two women watched in total silence as SSgt Brandert's long, slender fingers ran over the crease on a uniform, as she barked, "Every garment faces in the same direction, exactly one-half inch from the next garment!"

We all gathered around the locker, listening intently and not making a sound. No one dared to ask a question as we all seemed to already understand that we were there to listen and to do nothing else.

Next, we were shown the latrine and told that we would be required to keep it spic and span clean and that if we failed to do so the entire unit would be forced to do extra PT (Physical Training) each time the inspection turned up a defect. I didn't know what my fellow airmen were thinking as we heard all of this but I, for one, had already decided to do my best job every day. There is nothing worse in my book than being made to do extra chores because someone else screwed up and didn't do their chores properly. I am the youngest of seven children so I know what I'm talking about when it comes to doing someone else's chores.

Finally, all instructions had been received and we were told to hit the sack as Reveille, aka roll call, would be here before we knew it and we best be ready to start the day. At that moment, it began to really set in that I was not my own person anymore and that I now must take orders and ask permission before I could do anything. Basically, it felt a little like being stuck in a box and being told that you can only get out of the box when another person tells you to. That was the last thought I had before my eyes closed out of frustration and absolute exhaustion, as I had just endured one of the longest days of my life.

There is no way to describe how completely exhausted I was and how uncertain I was beginning to feel about my decision to join the United States Air Force. I really had no true idea of what being in the military would be like because my view was based on the letters my brother Jackson wrote to us. My mother read lots of his letters to me from the time I was a young girl until I got older. All I ever thought about growing up was joining the Air Force and getting a chance to travel and see the world the same way my brother had done during his military career. I never knew training would be so physically and mentally exhausting. I thought the Air Force was all about flying from one place to the next, meeting new people, and giving out a few orders to airmen who had to listen to you because you were in charge.

My mind was whirling as I drifted off to sleep trying to remember everything that had been said and trying to figure out if I had really made the right decision. Would life have been better back in Philly? Would I really have wound up just another teenage mother with no job prospects and no hope of getting married or going to college? I didn't know. How was I supposed to remember how far apart one uniform was supposed to be from the other? How was I to gauge the placement of my boots on the floor and make sure to arrange them at just the right distance and pointed in the right direction? And that bed, damn, I had just known it was too hard to fall asleep on. Damnit! I didn't know the answer to any of those questions, and those were the very last words to touch my lips as I drifted off to sleep.

BMTS in Full Swing

"GET UP! GET YOUR LAZY ASSES UP! NOW!"

We were awakened by more loud yelling as we were yanked out of bed, our bunks overturned, and ordered to stand at attention at the foot of our bunk for inspection before heading out for reveille. I could barely get my eyes open because I felt like I had just gone to bed, and now I was made to get up, stand alert, and listen to the instructions being yelled at me from what seemed like every direction. I tried to listen intently, and finally, I could make out that we better be in uniform and outside in the next 10 minutes or we would experience the full wrath of SSgt Brandert and Sgt Lopez.

SSgt Brandert and Sgt Lopez left just as suddenly as they had come in and all around me all I could hear and see was chaos. One girl was sitting on her cot just crying and rocking herself while another was just standing around in the middle of the room looking dazed and confused. Other than those two girls, everyone else was hustling like me, getting into uniform pants and shirt and trying to put those hard-ass boots on in less than 10 minutes and get outside as had been told. As I rushed towards the exit, I glanced sideways and noticed that the girl who had been standing around in a daze was now sitting next to the girl who was crying, and they were basically just holding each other and crying. As I took the stairs two at a time, I wondered what would happen to them and what that would mean for the rest of us. Would we be made to do more chores even though we hadn't done anything wrong or would those two just wind up getting into trouble all by themselves?

Suddenly, I was in line standing shoulder to shoulder with my fellow airmen, my mind a complete blank because I was completely focused on paying attention to the sergeants. I realized that I had gone into a little daze there and suddenly I was back as I heard our names being called one by one. I noticed that they stopped calling names suddenly when they didn't get a response for Connelly and Dempster. SSgt Brandert called "Connelly, Elaine" and "Dempster, Judith" one more time, and again there was complete silence. No one else spoke up either and out of the corner of my eye, I saw SSgt Brandert give an order to Sgt Lopez. She took off running into the barracks, presumably in search of Connelly and Dempster.

Sgt. Lopez returned in what seemed like seconds and whispered to SSgt Branderts. Then SSgt Brandert announced that Connelly and Dempster were being sent home after failing out of Basic Training.

"Listen up, they're the first and the last to go so don't anyone else get any other bright ideas. We only let two of you go without a fight, and they got lucky, but the rest of you are stuck here so you better get used to being in the United States Airforce," Brandert barked.

I didn't know what to think about all of that then. Should I have been happy for Connelly and Dempster and sad for myself or sad for Connelly and Dempster and happy for myself? One thing I knew for sure was that some hard shit was going to go down from this moment forward.

It's Getting Real

After reveille, we get a chance to go back to the barracks and fix up our beds and check out our uniforms to make sure that we'd be ready for inspection once we got back into formation. I had the chance to look in the mirror while I aligned my buttons with the clasp on my belt buckle so that everything was in a straight line, along with the zipper on my pants. Everything had to be absolutely perfect or else

SSgt Brandert would pull a 341 from your pocket and give you a write-up. The 341s are used to recognize when there is a discrepancy with your bunk, your boots, your uniform, or anything, but they're also used to notify you when you've done something correctly. I make a mental note to try to receive more 341s for doing something right than doing something wrong. The more positive 341s I received, the better it would look for me in my quest to become a squad leader.

Back in formation now, as we're marched to records processing for ID checks and to sign more papers. I received my military ID card today and was disappointed that my picture was so unflattering because of the haircut; in addition, more paperwork was forced on me in the form of training manuals and personal medical documents. In-processing continued for the remainder of the week along with vaccinations for all types of diseases, such as typhoid fever, yellow fever, and some diseases I'd never heard of but was informed would be required depending upon where they shipped me out to after basic training. My arm was so sore after having received all those vaccinations but I passed all medical processing standards with flying colors so it turns out that I am a perfect specimen for the United States Air Force.

I also learned one of the chants during our first drill today. I liked how it sounded. We were taught how to march in unison while chanting "US Air Force, US Air Force, Break it on down, US Air Force, US—Air Force!" The cadence was like one, two, three, four; one two three, four, one-two, three-four, one, two, three, four, one, two – three, four. I know, it sounds monotonous, but you had to hear it to appreciate its beauty.

I also liked hearing the way the drill sergeants taught us how to march in unison as they chanted along in their thick Texas drawl, "Heel, two, three, four; Heel, two, three, four; Lean back, settle in, Heel, two, three, four." You don't hear the "h" in "heel," so it sounds like "eel," which sounded funny to me. They also chanted "up" at the end of every count, so it sounds like "two-up," "three-up," "four-up."

Finally, we got just an hour of down time and I decided to use the time to write my Mom but partway through the letter, once again I felt spacey and remembered one of the last times that my mother read a letter to me from my brother Jackson during his time at Clark Air Force Base in the Philippines. My brother described how different everything was in the Philippines. He wrote about the food; how high the mountains were and how green the landscape was at the foot of the mountains; how different the people looked from African Americans; how the language sounded melodic and unlike any language he had ever heard before; and he noted that he was very thankful that English was spoken there, which made it easier for him to hold conversations with the native people. He also talked about the women and how they catered to the men, unlike anything he had ever experienced before in his life. He said he was made to feel like a king in his own castle because he wanted for nothing. Whenever he woke from a good night's sleep or came home from duty, he always had warm slippers waiting for him and a meal was always prepared for him without waiting. His reflections made it seem like I could have that kind of life as well, with someone waiting on me hand and foot.

He sent a picture of himself in his uniform sitting beside a Filipino woman. I had never seen a Filipino and her skin looked so pretty and flawless. Her hair was perfectly straight yet swirled under on the ends like a soft wave; she had on a white mini-dress with white go-go boots and perfect white Rose earrings, so I guessed that they were out on the town. She didn't appear to have any makeup on, but her expression was one of quiet sincerity. She honestly looked as if she could see me way over in North Philly almost as if she knew my brother would be sending this picture home for me to see. She was so pretty.

I couldn't get over how perfect and poised she was as if she had stepped right out of a 1960s magazine cover, and I wondered how long it had taken her to get such a perfect look. Her eye makeup made her eyes seem so intense, and I think that's what made me feel like she could see me all the way over in Philly. It was a casual picture, so I can't give credit to a photographer as most pictures were probably taken by another airman hanging out at the club.

There was nothing "basic" about basic training. Everything we learned was very specific, from learning how to make your bunk, to how to hang up your clothes or shine your boots. Even the way we ate wasn't basic because the first meal of the day happened at o'dark thirty, which is earlier than I had ever eaten in my life, and we must gobble it down super quickly and get back out into formation for our first drill of the day. The days moved fast when you were tasked with learning something new every hour. I learned that I liked making my bunk and trying to see if I could bounce a quarter off it because the bedclothes were so taut.

I especially enjoyed learning how to fold my clothes so that everything would fit neatly in my footlocker. I became an expert at folding my t-shirts, so they'd come out nearly wrinkle-free: you lay the t-shirt out flat, front-side down, and then fold it over with the shoulders a quarter-way onto the back of the shirt so that both shoulder sleeves were touching and there was no gap in the middle of the shirt. You lay it out in thirds and then fold the up from the bottom in thirds and down from the top in thirds. To this day, I still fold my t-shirts, underwear, and socks in military fashion because it makes sense and it enables me to fit a lot of items neatly in one drawer or in my luggage. I also continue to make the tight corners on my bed because it makes me feel nice and secure when I go to sleep at night.

BMTS, First Week Down

So, far this has been the worst day ever and I'm only three days on Lackland Air Force Base in San Antonio, Texas. The day started out as usual, but it was the end of the day that I remember the most because I suffered from the worst headache I ever had in my life. We had completed our marching drills for the day, along with all classroom activities, and I was back in the barracks getting ready for bed when as soon as my head hit the pillow, I suddenly felt pain exploding on both sides of my head and I became hot all over. I started screaming and crying all at the same time. I vaguely remember there being a lot of people around me suddenly asking me what was wrong, but I couldn't get any words out, all I could do was scream.

At some point, I remember hearing SSgt Branderts' voice, and someone else lifted me up and took me to the infirmary. By the time I got to the infirmary things were starting to come into focus and I could feel the pain subsiding in my head. They laid me down, turned out the lights, and told me to lie quietly. I lay there for what seemed like a very long time but later I was told I was only in the infirmary for a couple of hours and then I was escorted back to the barracks.

The doctor diagnosed a migraine headache brought on by all the stress and anxiety I had been feeling since Day 1 of basic training. I shared with the doctor my strong desire to become a squad leader and told him that I was feeling extra pressure on that front because I knew I needed to receive a certain number of 341s for good behavior over bad behavior. He explained that whenever I felt pain and pressure building up in my head to let the drill sergeants know and they would excuse me from duty so that I could go and lie down in the barracks. I realized that my 341s made no difference, and did not protect me; in fact, there was no protection.

From the time I was 15 and had the forced miscarriage up to 35, I was desperately seeking approval from people in uniform and positions of power, all men. It didn't matter what experiences came out of that as I was focused only on approval. I looked to my brother Jackson, I looked to Matthews, I looked to any men in uniform or in positions of authority for acceptance.

A couple of days later I was participating in PT and just after the last push-ups and sit-ups were done, bam, I started to stand up and the room started swimming, and down I went, straight to the floor, holding my head trying not to let it explode. This time I knew exactly why I was having a migraine but it still didn't alleviate the pain exploding in my head. Thankfully, SSgt Brandert saw me as soon as I fell and she yelled at a few of my fellow airmen to help me over to the infirmary. Those migraines were no joke. I could be feeling great one minute and then in the very next minute my head would be pounding, light hurt my eyes and noises became deafening.

Eventually, the migraine symptoms began to lessen, with each occurrence becoming more and more benign until they stopped altogether. I was glad to make it through basic training without having to receive a medical discharge due to migraine headaches. Until I joined the Air Force, I never knew what a migraine was, let alone that I suffered from them.

No 341s for Me

The next day, SSgt Brandert called me into her office. As I stood at attention, she yelled "At ease!" She asked about how I was feeling and if I had recovered from the migraine sufficiently to resume my duties.

"Ma'am, Yes, ma'am, I have recovered."

"Airman Green, you are now the squad leader for the remainder of basic training. Report to the PX to get your ribbon and report back to the barracks ASAP."

I had been selected to be the squad leader and attained my green belt because of my exemplary performance on the field and in the classroom (all those 341s came in handy)! Airman Basic Green, Squad Leader of 3743 BMTS (Basic Military Training Squadron), Flight W079 reporting for duty. Naturally, there were a few airmen that were none too happy about me being selected for such an honor but they had to accept it; otherwise, they risked the wrath of the drill sergeants if they didn't take my commands to heart. Being a squad leader was held in high regard by the other drill sergeants; the squad leader was in a position of authority over the other recruits in the absence of the drill sergeant, which made it an envious position indeed. One person had been selected out of many recruits because that person did most things correctly within the unit. I had always gravitated towards positions of leadership and control and being a squad leader was very satisfying. The squad leader marches out first in front of the airmen to present the unit to all the higher-ups when marching in formation.

As squad leader, I had to make sure everyone presented correctly in uniform, the bay area was clean, lockers were inspection-ready every day, and a whole host of other duties.

Most importantly, I couldn't take myself too seriously and start acting as if I was the drill sergeant because that would mean losing the respect of my peers or even the title of squad leader. I liked being in charge and enjoyed the respect I received from my peers and from Sgts Brandert and Lopez.

Homesick

Today after reveille and breakfast, I received my first batch of letters from home. I had been writing to everyone day after day and was beginning to wonder if I would ever receive any mail. It seemed as if the mail took twice as long to get to me as my brothers' letters had taken to arrive in North Philly. The first letter I opened was from Mama Ruth and I started crying before I even read the darn thing. Just looking at my mother's perfect flowing l's, t's, and m's made me cry. Mama writes with her left hand, but I have never seen any other left-handed person whose penmanship was as perfectly legible and beautiful as hers.

Berthienna,

I hope my letter finds you well and in good spirits. I know how hard basic training can be as I remembered some of what your brothers went through based on their letters to me so I can only imagine how much different and maybe sometimes harder it might be for you and other females.

I am well and your sisters and brothers say, hi. Your niece Angelique is getting bigger by the minute as well as your nephew Anderson. Please be sure to write back so I know that you are really ok. Everyone at Freedom Theatre says hello and they all want to get a letter soon. This is very difficult for me having you so far away and not knowing how you are doing. I miss our time together in the evenings before I would go off to work. No one else folds up my tissues like you do ☺ All of the tissues you folded are gone. Here is a tissue with my lipstick on it so that you will have a piece of home. All my love, Mom.

She missed me folding up her tissues and putting them neatly in her purse before she went out to work the bar at the Inntowner Motor Hotel at Broad and Lehigh. None of my other sisters would help her get ready for work as that was always our special time together. I smiled as I remembered so clearly watching her put on her makeup, dabbing her lips after applying lipstick; the smell of the tissue with her lipstick on it always made me smile. When I was younger, I would always hold onto that one tissue until after she left for work, and then I would press my lips right in the same fold hoping a trace of lipstick would still be there, so I would smell like her when I went to bed. I remember doing that for Mama from the time I was 13 up until the time I graduated high school.

I quickly read through letters from Tiffany, Rodney, and my brother Jackson and made certain to save the best letter for last – the one from Davis. I saved Davis's letter until it was bedtime so I could drift off to sleep with his poems in my head. Davis was always writing me poems, and this letter was no exception.

Baby, my eyes long to see your beautiful face,

But when I wake up in the morning all I see is empty space

It seems like just yesterday we were rolling around in bed

Talking about the day that we would wed

Now everyday all I do is daydream of being next to you

And pray that you miss me as much as I miss you too

Stay true to your heart and don't fall in love with anyone down there

So that you can come back to me none the worse for wear.

You are my one and only true love,
Davis

Every letter from Davis opened with either a long poem or a short poem and sometimes all he sent was a poem; my heart would get so full that I would cry myself to sleep longing to be lying in bed with him holding me tight. Even though the poem was short I could still see him clear as day reading the words to me and then taking me in his arms for a long and beautiful kiss. Davis's letter continued telling me how lonely he was and how he had been working a lot of extra hours at Radio 437 on Chestnut Street so he could save up enough money to come and see me. He said he was working so much that he didn't have time to stop by the theatre as much, but he had seen Tiffany and Rodney a few weeks ago and they told him to tell me hi and that they would write soon. Davis started to tell me how he really misses making love to me and before I know it I am starting to get all hot and bothered just thinking about his lips on mine and his fingers and lips all over my body. He was the most magical lover I had ever had and when we were together there weren't enough words in the English language to explain how it felt to have him inside me. Damn! I missed that man. His words were all that I needed to take me off to sleep at night. Thank you, God, I thought to myself, for bringing Davis into my life. I needed his love more than ever as I was miles and miles from home.

Cadence
Basic Training continued with one day melding into the next. The first time out on the range was very unsettling, to say the least. SSgt Brandert called us outside to line up in formation, squad leaders in the front. All you could hear in the dorm were lockers clanging, lots of airmen grunting and sighing about being made to go out again in the 100+ degree temperatures. It was odd that we were being told to line up because classes were done for the day, which usually meant we could use the rest of the time to tighten up our lockers, spit-shine our boots and prepare for afternoon inspection.

But we all pounded down the stairs, some taking two stairs at a time, as we filed into lineup.

SSgt Brandert called out, "A-ten-shun! Forward March! To the left, to the left, to the left, right, left. Double-time, march!"

Suddenly we were off and running! Then SSgt Brandert started the running cadence call, one of the best I've heard so far.

"I don't know, but I've been told (we airmen repeat the phrase – "I don't know but I've been told"). "People want to know. People want to know. Who we are. Who we are. So, we tell them. So we tell them. We are the Airforce. We are the Airforce. Mighty, mighty Airforce. Mighty, mighty Airforce. Better than the Army. Better than the Army. Ground-pounding Army. Ground-pounding Army. Better than the Navy. Better than the Navy. Deck-swabbing Navy. Deck-swabbing Navy. Better than Marine Corps. Better than Marine Corps. Jarhead Marine Corps. Jarhead Marine Corps. Better than the Coast Guard. Better than the Coast Guard. Lazy, lazy Coast Guard. Lazy, lazy Coast Guard. We are the Airforce. We are the Airforce. Mighty, mighty Airforce. Mighty, mighty Airforce. Rough, tough Airforce. Rough, tough Airforce. Lean, mean Airforce. Lean, mean Airforce. Mighty, mighty Airforce. Mighty, mighty Airforce. United States Airforce. United States Airforce. The last of the cadences was followed by silence for the next few minutes and all you could hear were boots on the ground.

Suddenly, Airman Taggert started to call cadence, "I don't know but I've been told. I don't know but I've been told. SSgt Branderts getting old. SSgt Branderts getting old. I don't know but I've heard reports. I don't know but I've heard reports. Sgt Lopez is getting short. Sgt Lopez is getting short. Sound off! 1, 2. Sound off! 1, 2. Sound off! 3, 4. Sound off! 3, 4. Bring it on down. Bring it on down. 1, 2, 3, 4! 1, 2, 3, 4. 1, 2, 3, 4! 1, 2, 3, 4!"

I COUNT THE DARK

Everyone busted out laughing, even SSgt Brandert because her birthday was the day before, and Sgt Lopez was laughing because she really is short. She was even shorter than me and I was only 5' 4". She couldn't have been more than 4'10" or maybe 4'11" at best. The rest of the marching was done in silence and then finally we realized we were at the shooting range. Every airman was handed goggles and an M-16 assault rifle. SSgt Brandert showed everyone how to get down on the ground in a prone position with our M-16 propped up on stilts. We were told to close one eye, look through the site on the M-16, take a deep breath, hold it and pull the trigger to hit the target several meters away, anywhere from 80 – 300 yards or more.

We were given the opportunity to fire off multiple practice rounds and then the qualifying round to see how well we could shoot after our first time on the range. After my sixth round of practice shots, it was time for my qualifying round. I remember lying on the ground, placing my M-16 rifle in just the right position, then taking a deep breath, holding it, and slowly squeezing the trigger. In just one qualifying round I made sharpshooter with my M-16! It was easier to accomplish than I thought it would have been.

During basic training we sometimes had to do extra chores because an airman messed something up, but not me; I made it to graduation and with my green belt as I had promised myself I would. I made a lot of new friends along the way and I was thrilled to be a squad leader because that meant I got to be first in line to get saluted by SSgt Brandert and Sgt Lopez as we stood at parade rest during the graduation. Graduation removed the title of Airman Basic Green and I advanced to Airman Green. It was a promotion of sorts: previously I was AB Green and now I was Airman Green.

Graduation was sweet. All the squads in unit 3743 BMTS, Flight W079 showed up with serious spit shines on our boots, ribbons that we had won proudly displayed across our chests, creases in our pants, and shirt sleeves that could cut you just as soon as you look at them. And how perfectly we all marched onto the parade field for the Pass and Review unit inspection parade. I remembered vividly how proud I felt when the flag was raised, and we sang the National Anthem. I had to fight back the tears because I didn't want to break formation by wiping my eyes, so I sucked them back as best as I could. SSgt Brandert and Sgt Lopez were dressed in their best uniforms also with ribbons neatly displayed. It had taken a long time to get to this point, but it had been worthwhile. At that moment, North Philly, and all I had left behind were the furthest things from my mind.

    I knew then that I had made the right decision to enlist and that this was where I belonged. I was able to send a few letters to Mama Ruth and Davis and received letters back as well from mom, Davis, and Janis. Davis and I were planning on getting together once I get to my permanent base instead because visits weren't permitted at Lackland. Also, I volunteered to attend ABGD (Air Base Ground Defense) training right after basic training. My leadership skills made me a good candidate to attend the 2-week ABGD program and I was super excited to attend the training, even though it means that much more time away from Davis. I was confident that the next level of training would better prepare me to secure and defend military installations as well as prepare me for wartime conflicts that involve securing the base perimeter from outside threats carried out on our shores.

Kat and Mason, My Besties

A BGD Training got off to a great start. I learned how to approach a suspect hunkered down inside a closed structure and how to advance from the shoreline to the outside perimeter of a base barracks double-time without making a sound. I perfected my high-crawl and low-crawl technique, executing the maneuver quickly without bringing attention to myself no matter how much ground I must cover. During the training, we got a chance to unwind in a more relaxed environment and could even go to the NCO (Non-Commissioned Officers) club, which is where I learned to play a game called Cardinal Puff-Puff. I thought I had mastered the game, but that wasn't the case.

One of the only legal ways to wind down on base was to drink alcohol. A lot of people drank off-duty to pass the time and socialize. There were times in the NCO Club when I saw some airmen so drunk that they had to be carried out of the club. People engaged in drinking games on base as well, and on the surface, these games appeared harmless, but I didn't know that for certain. Generally, it's male airmen who participated in these games, but I decided that I would try it out and then maybe play it with my friends. Cardinal Puff-Puff is a drinking game that basically involves claiming: "I drink to the honorable Cardinal Puff-Puff for the first time tonight," before you take a sip of your drink, and then make a series of moves using the forefinger of your left and right hands and feet. Once you make these moves the first time, you start them all over again until you have downed your alcoholic beverage five times in a row. If you mess up anywhere along the process you must stop immediately, consume the remainder of the entire beverage, and then start the process all over again. The fact that most people mess up the first time around is what makes the game fun because it's hard to concentrate on which moves you are supposed to do and in what order while downing a glass of alcohol. You quickly find yourself laughing out loud when you mess up and must finish off a glass of tequila, vodka, or rum and everyone else in the game is laughing at you as well. I don't know of a single soul who didn't get drunk the first time around playing this game. You try taking five shots of a beverage in a row and see where it gets you?!

Cardinal Puff-Puff is a serious drinking game and not for the faint of heart or anyone for that matter who cannot hold their liquor. I proved that I could hold my liquor just as many times as I proved I couldn't hold my liquor, becoming so intoxicated that I would find myself just drunk having lost the game. But for the most part, I won, even if winning meant I was tipsy drunk. There really wasn't much to do on base for young airmen so drinking games became a favorite pastime.

I met Kat, or Kendra Elaine Thompson, as she was called, and "Mason" Terry Irene Hillsetter during ABGD training. They were in different squads during Basic Training so we didn't actually meet until we all wound up at ABGD training together. We became fast friends because we were all from big cities on the East Coast or in the Midwest. Kat was from New York City, I hailed from Philadelphia, and Mason was from Chicago, or Chi-town, as we called it. My girls Kat and Mason were always right by my side whenever we went to the NCO Club and sometimes, they played the game, and sometimes they didn't. Kat was a skinny, light-skinned black girl who had red freckles on her face and a gap between her two front teeth. I had never seen a black person with freckles before but I was told that my brother Jackson was born with freckles and that he was very light-skinned at birth and had red hair. Mason and I were curvier than Kat, with big boobs and hips, and we both had the same chocolate brown complexion. Since we looked so much alike, we were also closer than either of us was to Kat. Mason played Cardinal Puff more often than Kat. I really liked my friend Mason and respected her as well because she hooked herself up quickly with a pilot whereas neither Kat nor I had succeeded in hooking up with anyone seriously as we made our way through ABGD training. Mason told me that she and Timothy were going to get married right after they left ABGD training and get stationed at the same base. I was jealous of her because I was lonely without Davis by my side and it was going to be lonely at my next base without him. He couldn't leave Philly, his grandmother, and his entire family just to come and live in Texas with me.

Soon we found out that Kat, Mason, and I were all going to be stationed at Dyess AFB together. As it turned out Mason's "Timothy" was going there as well, so she was psyched to know that they would not be separated after all. I was so happy to know that I would have someone at Dyess that I already knew.

Airman Green

> *We may encounter many defeats*
> *but we must not be defeated.*
> -Maya Angelou

DYESS AFB, Abilene, Texas
28-12-79

Arrived at the base early on a Friday morning in 1979 and began my journey as Airman Green, LE (Law Enforcement), stationed on one of the largest S.A.C. (Strategic Air Command) bases in Texas. I successfully finished almost 280 hours of basic training and an additional two weeks of Air Base Ground Defense training to finally be shipped out to DYESS AFB, which is located about 7 miles southwest of Abilene, Texas, and 180 miles west of Dallas, Texas. SAC bases at that time had control of land-based strategic bomber aircraft and intercontinental ballistic missiles or ICBMs.

My daily duties consisted of rising early, attending reveille, straightening up my barracks/locker and boots, reporting to duty at the armory to pick up my weapon, and then reporting to my post. I was the only female, black female in a unit that consisted of mostly white men, a few Hispanics, and a couple of other black airmen as well. Since I was the only female and one of the only airmen that could type well, I was chosen to be the dispatcher on duty with the responsibility of dispatching my fellow law enforcement personnel to handle situations on base involving all non-commissioned officer personnel. That did not sit well with some of the men, but they couldn't type, so there was nothing they could do about it.

Being the dispatcher on duty placed me in an 'unofficial' position of authority. In this position, I was responsible for typing up all the reports and forwarding them to the TSgt Alameda on duty for review. What I did not know at the time but that I believed was possible, is that the men in my unit resented me for having that responsibility. The dispatcher position is usually reserved for Sgts and above and not for little AIC's like me. This is also probably why I went on my three-day breaks with another unit that had more black airmen and a wonderful older man I called 'Sarge'. Sarge was a really nice man with a hearty laugh. Physically, he reminded me of what my grandfather might have looked like as a younger man with his full mustache, long arms, and long fingers.

My unit was responsible for handling drunk and disorderly conduct issues, breaking and entering's, fights, domestic disturbances, and even suicides on base. Basically, any situations that took place on-base we were responsible for handling could lead to just being locked up for one night or advancing all the way to being out-processed with an Article 15 discharge due to the severity of the situation. There were many days and nights when I typed up numerous reports involving other airmen and non-commissioned officers being handcuffed and brought to the station to be charged with one crime or another.

As a law enforcement officer, I had responsibility for maintaining law and order within the perimeter of the base and apprehending the alleged guilty parties, and later processing the required paperwork to charge them with a crime. Yet, when my crimes were reported, to my knowledge, there was never a real investigation. I became yet another invisible cog in the wheels of justice. Where was justice when I needed her most? Nowhere to be found. Many victims of sexual assault go unnoticed in society today for many reasons, only one of which is due to system failure.

I can remember watching airmen puke next to each other as they were handcuffed to the railing just outside the dispatch station before they were taken away for processing. Most of the altercations that led to being arrested involved drunk and disorderly because there just wasn't much to do on base other than getting drunk.

I often wondered how many of my fellow airmen returned home as full-fledged drunks with alcoholism as a primary deterrent to obtaining a decent job and maintaining a family life. I witnessed way too many men spend their 3-day breaks drinking from the beginning to the end of their 72-hour breaks in our 9-day rotating shifts. It is my opinion that during the late 1970s and early 1980s, the Airforce was a breeding ground for alcoholism back then. Every airman on a 3-day break, at one time or another, may have consumed alcohol as a form of recreation. Because we arrested enough airmen for drunk and disorderly conduct on every shift, that certainly indicated that drinking was a way of relaxing off shift. I cannot recall most airmen being disciplined harshly for drunk and disorderly conduct.

All the shifts for the units were typically broken out into 3 days, 3 mids (3pm to 11pm), and 3 nights (midnight to 7 am) rotating. I actually liked the 9-day rotations because they definitely broke up the monotony of my shift. Yet, at the same time, I eagerly looked forward to each 72-hour break because my fellow airmen and I would always go someplace different on our 3-day breaks. We would take trips to practically every city in Texas just to have someplace to go during our off time. It was during one of these 3-day breaks that I had my first taste of marijuana.

My friends Kat and Mason (Terry) jumped in Terry's boyfriend's car one 72-hour break and decided to drive to Dallas for some fun. During the way, we stopped at a 7-11 somewhere along a Texas highway and Kat went inside to get us some drinks and snacks. Kat came back to the car grinning but without the drinks and snacks and Terry and I, both asked her, "What's up? Where's the stuff?" Kat asked, grinning like a Cheshire cat from ear to ear, "the guy at the counter asked me out of the clear blue sky if we wanted some weed to go along with our snacks and I said sure just let me go and talk it over with my friends."

According to Kat, he was practically giving it away because he said he had too much and no way to sell it all before his shift is over, so he basically wanted to just give it to us.

So, naturally, we told Kat, "Shit, if he's giving it away, go back in there and get the stuff and come on. Let's get out of here before a bunch of cops suddenly show up out of nowhere looking to arrest a couple of dumb airmen looking to score some weed."

Kat went back in and came back out in a flash and we drove off to Dallas and booked into our motel room.

Once we were in the motel room, I found out that both Terry and Kat had smoked weed before, so they were totally comfortable with crumbling the weed up into the rolling papers and rolling them into these tight little cigarette-like joints. I watched them both with intense scrutiny as they rolled 5 joints and then it was time to light one and begin smoking. Kat lit the first joint and sucked it hard until it seemed to me that she was going to suffocate herself from the outside pulling in all that smoke at once and then holding it in for a couple of seconds until finally, she blew out this large puff of smoke hard. I was stunned, surprised, and shocked all at the same time.

Next, she passed the joint to Terry and Terry did the same thing and then the two of them burst out laughing, at nothing it seemed to me at the time.

Suddenly, it was my turn and I took hold of the joint and timidly pulled it close to my lips and attempted to try to suck on it without putting it to my lips and quite naturally I failed to suck in any smoke, Terry rolled her eyes.

"No, not like that." She grabbed it from me. "You have to put your lips on it and open your mouth a little and then suck in the smoke."

"Ok," I said, "let me try it again."

So, this time I placed the joint between my lips and parted my lips a little, and sucked in the smallest amount of smoke. Before I knew it, I was choking and gagging all over the place and not feeling very good at all. My throat and chest felt like it was on fire, and I had hardly done anything. Terry took the joint and passed it to Kat and they kept passing it back and forth amongst themselves until the first joint was totally burnt out.

As they lit the second joint I spoke up and said… "Ok, let me try it again."

I had watched them for the last 10 minutes, so I felt as if I could do it this time. Kat lit the joint, took a drag, and then passed it to me. I placed the joint to my lips and once again took a drag myself. It was a short drag but this time I held it in for a couple of seconds before I blew it out and started coughing again but this time the coughing was not as bad. The rest of the night was pretty much a blur, but I do remember that once we finished smoking that joint, we went out to one of the clubs in Dallas and drank up a good little bit of mixed drinks and made our way back to the motel safely.

The rest of our 72-hour break was pretty much just more of the same and by the end of our break, I can tell you that I was a full-fledged pot smoker for the first time at the ripe old age of 19. My, oh, my how different my life suddenly was from that little girl from North Philly. I'm sure this was not what my mother intended for me when she sent me off to 'protect and defend my country with my life.' Here I was, formerly miss goody-two-shoes and all, out breaking the law. I did it and didn't feel bad about doing it either. I think

I was just trying to show off some of my North-Philly-street cred to match my girl Kat from NYC and Terry from Chi-town. Most likely, but either way, it made me feel good. Finally, I was able to really enjoy my 3-day breaks with friends instead of always feeling shut out by the men in my unit. I always follow the rules, but I was learning quickly that following the rules does not always lead to friendships.

From Afro to Bouffant

The days went by fast, quickly becoming weeks and months at Dyess, AFB, but no matter how fast the days went past, nothing in Abilene ever prepared me for how to take care of my hair in that dry, desert-like landscape. One of the worst things for a young, black girl like me was no longer having the ability to do my hair in as many different styles as I used to be able to in the past. My hairstyles were very limited because of the severe butch-like haircut I received and the hair growth I experienced after basic training.

I can still remember the first time I tried out one of the hair salons in Abilene, Texas, because I was just desperate to have my hair washed to get some of that red dirt out of my hair. Terry's boyfriend had a car and she convinced him to let her borrow it to drive me to the hair salon. I had no idea how my hair was going to turn out, but I was convinced that anything had to be better than the smushed-down afros I was sporting day after day on base.

We drove to the salon and the first thing I noticed was that all the women in there were white and they had high bouffant hairdos with pins sticking all over their heads. Now that should have been enough to cause me to turn tail and run but noooo, no I just had to have my hair washed so I sat down in the chair. And, let me tell you how wonderful it felt to have that warm water swooshing all thru my hair and to have someone else's fingers running through it. Dang, that shampoo and conditioner felt wonderful.

Now when the stylist asked me, "Ok hon, how do you want your hair?"

Well, I knew that I couldn't say just a 'press n curl' because I didn't know if they would even know what that meant so I just said, "Give me whatever is new and stylish so that I will look good."

Well, why did I say that?! The stylist proceeded to part my hair in sections and put these really big curlers on them with pins and set me under the dryer.

After I came out of the dryer, she started teasing my hair and plying me with hairspray repeatedly. She said that I needed a lot of hair spray to hold my hair up on these hot Texas days and nights. I said. "Uh hmmm, ok."

Finally, I was done, and she turned me around and put the mirror in my hand.

Honestly, I can't remember what I said, but I paid and ran out of the salon trying frantically to push my hair down, down, down from its four-foot crown. Terry looked at me and bust out laughing as she drove away from the salon back to base. I knew without a doubt that I had the highest bouffant hairdo known to man and most definitely the highest bouffant hair doo any little girl from North Philadelphia has ever seen. I had to laugh at myself just a little as well because I can't believe I was so dumb and desperate to waste my money like that but at least now I know better. I ran inside and couldn't wait to drench my head in water and shampoo to get out all that hair spray. I learned a most valuable lesson that day. Not all hair salons are the same down south and the east coast is far, far away from Abilene, Texas.

Thinking back on life on Dyess AFB and the surrounding areas there really were not that many places for black women to go and get their hair done. Most of the salons catered to white hair. The stylist probably rarely encountered a black woman coming into the shop much less a young, black woman with a hair texture that was much different from the mostly straight-haired white clients they were used to servicing. Being in the military back then, black women kept their hair stuffed up under their caps most of the time which is why a lot of pictures of me back then show these weird tufts of hair smashed down looking as if my hair had no body whatsoever.

Whenever I ran into other black female airmen, I often asked them what they do with their hair after they wash it to try to keep it soft. Most brought jars of Dixie Peach or Royal Crown with them from home and just did the best they could to keep it braided most of the time. The black airmen never seemed to really mind our hair so much back then which is interesting as I think about it now. Today hair is a big deal and we have so many different hairstyles to choose from to manage our crowns.

Most of the white female airmen seemed to have no problems with their wash-n-go hair so they probably only went to the salon for a time. Most of my interactions on base were with as many black airmen and NCOs that I could find making it completely different from basic training. In basic training, I made a lot of friendships with the white girls on Lackland AFB; however, life on Dyess AFB was almost completely different. You see, I was deep in Texas where they believed in playing heavy metal music as loud as possible and where most activities were not geared toward black people. We had to drive out of Abilene and head towards Dallas, Texas to find some jazz music or Rhythm and Blues. On base, almost every race kept to themselves when it came to socializing although we would protect each other with our lives if it came down to it in wartime.

Time Keeps On Slipping . . .

Music playing low in the background… "Fly Like An Eagle" …. "Time keeps on slipping, slipping, slipping, into the future. Time keeps on slipping, slipping, slipping, into the future. I wanna fly like an eagle …to the sea….Fly like an eagle ….Let my spirit carry me….I want to fly like an eagle….Till I'm Free….Oh, Lord, through the revolution."- Steve Miller Band …..one of my favorite songs from the past was playing as I walked into the NCO club on base. Out on the dance floor was a very handsome man who noticed me just as quickly as I noticed him. He finished his dance and started walking over to me.

This very handsome, light-skinned, black man introduced himself to me as SSgt Keith Davis. He walked up to me as I was sitting with Terry and Kat having a drink and asked if he could join me. I must admit that he was juicy looking in his uniform with his muscles bulging all over the place and I had a chance to catch his nice ass as he went to go get me another tequila sunrise from the bar. He also had this really nice deep but soft voice that made me want to kiss him every time his lips parted, and I had a chance to see his shiny perfect teeth.

Everything started out nice and sweet with Keith as we got to know each other over the next few weeks and months. I had some real street credo now because I was dating a SSgt. That was a sign that I was special in my book dating someone of a higher rank is great. In a way, it elevated my status to be hanging out with Keith. Things were going along so well that when I told Keith that I didn't know how to drive a car he went out and bought a car just to teach me how to drive.

I remembered one Saturday when Keith was knocking hard on my door. Rubbing the sleep out of my eyes, I yelled, "Who is it?"

"Get dressed and come outside."

Sometimes his bossiness could be so irritating, but the other times, he came across as the most gentle and kindest person you could ever want to meet. He was a natural-born leader, and he was used to getting his own way because he had been a SSgt for almost five years. When you are in a position of ordering people around, sometimes it can go to your head, and you start to feel entitled to getting your own way all the time.

I dressed quickly and ran outside to witness Keith grinning at me and pointing to a maroon car, holding the keys. You could've lit up the darkest night as you watched the smile on my face grow wider and wider. In two steps, I was in his arms, holding him tight, and he whispered in my ear, "This is all yours, baby!" Then he said, "Come on, let's go for a ride." It was a stick shift, which was different from an automatic but interesting to learn how to drive. Every time I moved my foot from the clutch, brake, and accelerator I felt like I was in a go-cart from back home.

Keith was an experienced driver; he got behind the wheel and drove us off-base to a patch of dry land just outside of the base. We switched seats. Keith pointed to the brake, clutch, and gas pedal, telling me when to use each pedal. There were beads of sweat forming on my upper lip and my forehead as I put my foot on the pedals and the car lurched forward. I quickly moved my foot to the brake and the car cut off. Keith sighed, looked me dead in the eye in the most eerily calm voice, and said, "Try it again." Letting out a deep sigh, I adjusted my cap and tried it again and again until I was finally driving down the road. I almost yelled it out to the world, "I'm driving a stick shift!'

Quiet Intensity

I was in awe of him to a certain extent because here I was a little black girl from North Philly with my man Davis still at home whom I still considered my boyfriend and yet here I was with this older guy wanting to buy me anything and everything and we had only shared a kiss or two here and there. I didn't know what to expect and I must admit that in reflection I was very naïve to think that I wouldn't have to 'pay up' in some way for his kindnesses but that's who I was at the time. I had never had this kind of attention before from anyone other than Davis so in a way it was kind of exciting.

Keith was very reserved, and quiet yet also somewhat demanding in how he spoke to me. It was never 'Do you want to do such-n-such but rather-Come on we are going to do this now.'

Though I knew it was permitted to date Sgts (or higher-ranking officers) on base so long as they were not your direct superiors, I was made increasingly uncomfortable by Keith pressuring me to have sex with him. I kept saying no. He decided that since I wouldn't give him any sex there was no reason to keep the car, which he said he had bought for me. He told me I could no longer drive it and had to give him the keys back so he could sell it. Around that time, I decided to break up with him because I wasn't about to have sex with him since I was still in love with Davis.

The images that come to mind of Keith mostly reflected a tall, strong black man with a gentle disposition. At times he could be a little abrupt and commanding; however, I attributed that to his position of command being a SSgt in the Airforce for the last five years or more. I knew that to be a leader you must exude a sense of authority in front of your units so that you wouldn't be taken advantage of and so the airmen would follow your command, so when he came off a little abrupt with me, I mostly shook it off. I took his kindness for just friendship and was naïve enough to believe that that's how he meant it to be so when he took the car back, I was stunned. I never really thought of him as the possessive type just caring and conscientious about me having a good time while stationed on base. In retrospect, I now see how badly I misjudged his kindnesses.

One day, after we had already stopped talking to each other, Keith invited me back to his room because he said he wanted to talk and apologize for selling the car so abruptly. I decided to go and hear what he had to say even though Terry was telling me to just leave it alone and let him go and be done with everything.

I met him in his room and he offered me a soda and we started to talk. Before long Keith leaned in to kiss me, and I pushed him back saying, "No, let's not do this again, it's over."

Keith looked at me, hurt and confused. He said, "I thought that we could maybe get back together and that everything would be okay?"

I said, "No, it's over, and it has nothing to do with the car it's just over."

Keith stood up and grabbed me with both arms, shaking me and forcing his lips onto mine. "You're mine and nothing's gonna change that," he growled.

I struggled, trying to get loose of his grip. Just then there was a knocked at the door and someone called his name. "Keith. Hey Keith, come on man."

Before I could say a word, Keith clamped his hand over my mouth and in one quick motion lifted me up, all 128 lbs. and 5' 4" inches of me, carried me to his wall locker, threw me inside, and slammed the door. I felt like a small stuffed panda bear that an angry little kid picks up and throws into his closet when he doesn't want to play with it anymore. Where did this behavior come from suddenly? Keith had never said an unkind word to me in the past and he had never put his hands on me. When he picked me up, I felt the full weight of his strength and knew that he could overpower me in seconds flat and do whatever he wanted to do to me to get satisfaction. He lifted me up as if I was nothing more than a rag doll.

The next thing I knew he was out the door and I was stuck inside his locker. His strength at that moment totally surprised me. I knew he was strong because I'd seen him lift a lot of weight in the gym, but he still shocked me, nonetheless. I can't even recall how all of this happened so quickly. Minimal encoding, remember that phrase from earlier? I do know that as soon as I collected my wits, I set out to get out of that locker. My head, back, and shoulders hit the cold, hard metal of the locker causing me to wince in pain. I blinked back tears as I realized that I was actually in his locker. I felt the sharp creases of his uniform give way under my weight. I could feel my breath pounding in my ears as I tried to slow my breathing and gather my thoughts to get out of there before he returned.

I kept pushing on the lock and pushing on the door until it slammed open and I half fell out of the locker and ran out of his room. I put my ear to his door to listen for sound, hearing none, I opened the door to get out of his room so quickly that I barely looked to see if he was standing in the hall. There was no one in the hallway so I ran quickly down the hall, into the stairwell, down one floor to my room. I cried all the way to my room realizing that I was in shock as to what had just occurred. I don't know what would have happened had that guy not come along and called out to him, but I do know that I was scared.

The next morning, I asked to see the base commander and reported what had happened. The commander's outer office was pristine, with chairs pushed up close to the wall, one wood table in the middle of the room with magazines displayed for reading by civilians, as uniformed personnel was not allowed to sit and peruse magazines, but rather we were meant to stand at parade rest while waiting to be called

I COUNT THE DARK

into the commanders' office. The intercom buzzed, the secretary whispered something that I could not hear clearly, released the button, and motioned for me to enter the commander's office. I marched into the commander's office and raised my right hand to salute the commander. Almost immediately the commander returned my salute and instructed me to stand at parade rest. "Airman Green, state your case."

I took a deep breath and began to tell the commander the events that transpired the night before being careful to identify the time, date, location, and names of all individuals involved. The commander asked me a few questions to which I responded and then dismissed me, instructing me to return to duty posthaste. My nerves were raw as I walked back to my post and resumed my duties. My hands shook as I was handed my weapon at the armory. I scanned my weapon and holstered it ASAP and reported to duty.

The commander told me that I would be called down to see him again after the investigation was conducted to determine what had happened and that I would be notified of the results of the investigation. I left the whole situation alone and continued with my life reporting to duty and taking my three-day breaks. My conversations with Davis started back up again, and he announced that he was coming to visit me for the Memorial Day holiday at the end of May. I was so excited to have the opportunity to see him and reconnect because it had been a long time since we had seen each other. As I prepared for Davis's arrival, I forgot all about the situation with Keith Davis, and it never even dawned on me that he was suddenly no longer a problem. I figured that he was given a stern talking-to by the base commander and that he was given an order to leave me alone which he followed to the letter.

Approximately three weeks later, my direct superior, TSgt Alameda, called me into his office to inform me that the investigation had been concluded and that the determination was that there was no proof of assault. SSgt Keith Davis was interviewed and based upon the lack of evidence and the testimony of SSgt Davis; the investigation was closed. SSgt Davis was processed out to Andrews AFB effective immediately and I was instructed to acknowledge that the case had been closed to everyone's satisfaction.

As I listened to the words coming out of TSgt Alameda's mouth, tears started to form in my eyes, my chest was getting tight and I felt like I couldn't breathe. TSgt Alameda released me instructing me to go to chow and then report back to duty tomorrow morning at 0700 hours. What surprised me the most with this entire ordeal is that I was not given a chance to defend my side of the attack. I did not go to chow and instead chose to go straight back to my barracks. I half walked-ran back to my room opening and slamming the door so quickly that I thought the door would break.

In my anger, I popped a button off my uniform as I took it off and fell onto my bunk, crying, and pounding the pillow, thinking to myself, this is why I have not seen SSgt Davis around – because he is no longer here on base. I was beginning to see the Airforce in a new light. It no longer seemed as if this was a safe place for me, the place my mother thought would protect me from the mean streets of North Philly. Never had I found myself in a situation like what happened with SSgt. Davis.

In the past, if something bad happened everyone believed my truth and not someone else's. I suddenly started to feel very small and weak, no longer the strong, proud girl from a tough neighborhood in Philly. I curled up, fists bawled, breathing heavily, and cried myself to sleep. I was awakened several hours later by a knock on my door. Opening the door, I saw Kat and Mason looking at me with concern. Kat sighs, saying, "We heard about the results of the investigation."

Mason chimed in, embracing me in a hug saying, "How are you? Get dressed, and let's go eat. We can talk about this over dinner."

Mason had borrowed her boyfriend's car, so we drove off base and had dinner at the Sizzlers buffet up the road.

Surprisingly, I was starved and so I stuffed my face full of steak, baked potato, green beans, chocolate cake, and as much watermelon as I could stand. In a few short hours, I felt better and knew that I had no choice but to accept the commander's decision and at least be glad about the fact that I would not have to see SSgt Davis on base anymore. As I ate, I reflected on the decision made in my situation. It seemed to me that it was no different than saying that I must have made up the whole tale about the assault. The base commander chose to believe the words of SSgt Keith Davis over me and rewarded him with his BOP to Andrews AFB that he had been waiting on for a while. The veil was being removed: that picture-perfect sunny Airforce base experience was slowly becoming cloudy and grey.

The 24-Hour Engagement

Days passed by quickly as I was awaiting Davis's arrival and finally, May 23rd arrived and Davis was there. We booked a motel in downtown Dallas-Fort Worth to be able to spend some alone time together for the weekend. We started out just staring at each other, him looking at me in my uniform and me looking at him in his shiny new Chrysler Cordoba with that rich Corinthian leather, as Ricardo Montalban liked to say in the commercials. That car was so shiny, and Davis purposely bought one in my favorite color, hunter green. We spent a short time on base while I introduced him to Terry and Kat and we hung out in my room for a short time just talking about life in Philly and his drive down to Texas. I planned a week's vacation to coincide with Davis's drive down to Texas to pick me up but first, we were going to spend the night in the motel in Dallas-Fort Worth before getting on the road back to Philly. This was going to be my first cross-country trip, so I wanted us to be as well-rested as possible. Terry and Kat left, and we said our goodbyes since I would be leaving the next day to drive back home to Philly. Finally, we were alone together and able to express how much we had missed each other. Let me tell you, writing letters and phone calls is nothing compared to seeing each other in the flesh. And, speaking about flesh, it only took us a few minutes, but it felt like seconds before we had our clothes off and were making love in my bunk just like old times.

We only had time for a quickie but it was absolutely fabulous after being apart for so long. I don't remember what we said to each other because every other word was quieted with kisses and promises to never be apart so long ever again. After what seemed like hours, but was only 30 minutes, we pulled ourselves out of bed, used the bathroom, and grabbed my suitcase before heading out the door to make the drive to the motel in Dallas Fort Worth.

The motel was as nice as motels can be and we had stopped along the way to grab a bite to eat and snacks for the night. Once we got to the motel, I went to the bathroom to freshen up and left Davis to figure out what was on TV. When I came out, I was stunned to see that somehow Davis had decorated the bed with rose petals and he was kneeling at my feet as soon as I stepped out of the bathroom. Davis looked up at me with a big smile on his face and said, "Just stop. Stand still and let me look at you."

Smiling, I tried to step past him saying, "What are you doing?"

Looking over his shoulder, first I noticed the flowers because they were all over the place and they were so beautiful.

Davis then pulled me back in front of him and took both my hands in his hands, looking back up at me saying, "Bubblegum! My sweet Tina girl, I have missed you so much. I wake up every morning thinking of you, and throughout the day, I wonder what you must be doing at this very moment."

Taking his face in my hands, I knelt and kiss him ever so gently, passionately whispering, "I have missed you too, babe. You just don't know how much I have missed you."

Davis's hand touches the small of my back as he pulls me closer to him and whispers in my ear. "Tina, will you marry me?"

Pulling back, eyes glazing over with tears, a smile as wide as the Mississippi begins to spread across my face, and I scream. "Yes! Yes! Yes! I will marry you, Jeffrey D. Russell."

A moment this momentous required the use of Davis's full name. Lifting his hands to my cheek and taking my face in his hands.

He placed the ring on my finger, and we held each other and kissed for the longest time. I was crying happy tears and kept kissing his neck, his lips, his cheeks, just all over his face. I was happier than I had ever been in my life, just knowing that I would spend the rest of my life with my soulmate. I had forgotten all about Dyess AFB, my unit, my friends, SSgt Keith Davis, everybody. All I could think about was the life that we were going to have, how the military would fit into our lives, where we would live, etc.

We both finally got up off the floor and made our way to the bed to begin the most passionate lovemaking that either of us had ever felt in life before. As the night progressed, all I could do was stare at the diamond on my finger, smiling languidly as my eyes began to softly close as Davis and I cuddled in each other's arms and drifted off to sleep.

No Ring, No Fiancé
Davis and I woke up early the next morning and got on the road for our drive back to Philly. We were making good time and stopped for another overnight stay on the way back home. Two days later, as we were driving along the road, we decided to pull into a rest stop so that we could get more gas and snacks and so I could go to the bathroom. We got back on the road and about one hour into our drive I looked down at my left hand and noticed that my ring was gone.

I screamed and Davis almost lost control of the car trying to figure out what was wrong. I just started crying and thru my tears, I told him that I lost my ring realizing that I had taken it off just to wash my hands in the bathroom at the rest stop and I did not realize until just now that I never put the ring back on my finger. Davis was as devastated as I was and quickly tried to find an off-ramp so that we could go

I COUNT THE DARK

back to the rest stop to see if anyone had turned in my ring. I was hoping for the best, but I had a sinking feeling that no one would have turned it in.

Davis was quiet most of the ride back to the rest stop but occasionally he would ask me, "Why did you take it off?"

My response was the same every time he asked, I simply did not want to get it dirty with soap getting caked up on my ring, and I wanted to keep it shiny. Dumb response for a 19-year-old girl, I know, but it was how I felt at the time. I only had my ring for a little over 24 hours, and already it was gone. Of course, by the time we reached the rest stop, and I ran quickly into the bathroom, the ring was nowhere to be found. Davis and I both tried to find a guard or someone to ask about a lost and found, but once we found a guard, she said that no one had turned in any jewelry. Somehow, we made the best of it and finally arrived back in Philly with a few days left to spare before I had to return to base. I went from being so happy to share the good news with my mother, family, and Tiffany to being totally embarrassed and unable to tell anyone that we were engaged.

Davis and I tried to have a good time together during the rest of the ride home but by the time we arrived in Philly we were barely talking, except, for the obligatory, good morning and pass the fries please whenever we stopped to eat. My arrival home was overshadowed by our failed engagement. I couldn't even enjoy my time at home because I could tell as the days went by that Davis was more upset than he let on initially.

Auntie

Davis called later the next day and asked me to meet him at his grandmother's house after he got off work so we could talk. As I sat waiting for 4 o'clock to come so I could catch the 52 to go over to his grandmother's house, all I could think about was him. I saw his handsome face everywhere I turned, and silent tears filled my eyes as I thought of our broken engagement. While standing waiting for the bus I glanced down at my left hand and saw how ashy and barren my hand looked. Exhaling loudly, I reached in my purse, found my lotion, and squirted out a dime-sized dollop rubbing it onto my hands.

The bus came quickly, I stepped on, paid my fare, and sat down. Looking around at the other passengers my gaze fell on a couple sitting together about four seats away on the right side of the bus. I could tell by their body language that they were a couple. She had her head resting on his shoulder and I wondered would Davis and I ever sit like that again. My thoughts turned inward as the bus lurched forward pulling away from the bus stop as I thought of what I would say to Davis.

Before I knew it, I was at 52nd and Market streets and I pulled the buzzer to alert the driver that I wanted to get off. That day the walk to his grandmother's house was the longest walk of my life although she only lived a block and a half away from the bus stop. I rang the doorbell and before I could check my reflection in the screen door, Davis opened the front door. Smiling we both leaned in to kiss each other and I stepped inside. As usual, there are blue and gold pillows scattered all over the gold sofa which was encased in plastic. The sofa always seemed to let out a little sigh whenever you sat on it as if to say 'hi, you are welcome to sit on me'.

The living room is small and cramped. Besides the sofa there is one other green upholstered chair that sits in the corner with a small organ beside that, followed by an end table and then a brown coffee table that sits in the middle of the floor. Davis takes my hand and we head towards the stairs up to his room. I slip my hand out of his just long enough to run into the kitchen and give Auntie a hug. Everyone calls his grandmother 'Auntie' although I have never really known why that is, I began calling her that also from the moment Davis and I started dating.

Auntie was one of the nicest women that I have ever known, and she truly loved me and was the strongest advocate that Davis and I had for being a couple. She was always telling him, 'I don't know why you don't go on and marry her, you know you two belong together.' As Auntie turned to greet me a deep smile spread across her face and she said 'you staying for dinner girl? 'Smiling back at her and pulling her in for a big hug and a peck on the cheek, I said, maybe, and scooted back over to the stairs to grab Davis's hand and head on upstairs.

Davis was waiting for me on the stairwell. I slipped my hand in his and we proceeded up the stairs. Leaning over the banister, he locked eyes with Auntie and said-you can just cover up the food when it's done and we will come back down a little later to eat.

In a flash, we were up the stairs and, in his room, which was located in the rear of the house. His tiny bedroom always made me feel safe and secure because it was so comfy. The wallpaper had gold flowers on it and was peeling yet this still felt like my second home. The only place to sit was on the bed because the dresser, brown lamp, black table, and twin-sized bed took up most of the room. However, one wall was dedicated to his turntable, equalizer, speakers, subwoofer, albums and cassette tapes galore. Davis was the best D.J. I knew and he was always mixing tapes for me filled with love songs and fast thumping beats.

I sat on the bed as Davis moved to the turn table, picked out an album, Winelight by Grover Washing, Jr., and started playing 'Just the two of us' real low on the turntable. Turning to sit down on the bed, I could tell by the downward turn of his eyes that he was having trouble with what he wanted to say. I want to talk to you about how I feel, he said. Reaching for his hand and looking up into his eyes, I said. I know, me too. Davis reached up his right hand to touch the left side of my cheek and a tear fell and landed on the back of his hand. I leaned into the palm of his hand and he said, "You know I love you, but I am having difficulty dealing with the loss of the ring. I mean, I haven't finished paying for it and I still can't believe you lost it."

More and more tears fell with every word he spoke, and he continued to gently wipe them away. I tried my best to straighten up and stop crying but it was hard. Whispering, "I'm so sorry. I can't believe that I lost it either. All I remember is not wanting to get soap all over it and dirty it up. I wanted that ring to shine, shine, shine."

Wiping more tears from my eyes, he says, "I know you didn't mean to but it still hurts. I just wish we could have found it when we drove back to the gas station but somehow, I knew it wasn't going to be there. I mean who doesn't want to pick up a diamond ring just sitting there on the sink. Damn! Babe, it makes me wonder if that was a sign."

I wanted to lean into him so bad, but something was stopping me. All I could say was "What kind of a sign?"

Looking down, Davis said, "Maybe it's a sign that we are not meant to be together."

My eyes widened in a look of total surprise. "Why would you think that after all that we have been through? It's not a sign of anything other than my carelessness. Babe, you have got to know that we belong together. A ring does not change what we feel for each other."

Davis pulled me in and hugged me tight. Burying my face in the softness of his sweater, pulling in all his musty Jovan scent, I mumbled that I wanted to marry him and spend the rest of my life raising our babies, playing music, and building a life together.

Brushing my hair softly, he pushed me away from him just long enough for me to see the tears building in his eyes, his long lashes blinking rapidly to stop the flow. Davis looked at me silently for what seemed like the longest time as I stared into his deep brown eyes. After a while, he said, "That's what I want more than anything."

Then without words, we began to undress each other and make love in silence. Orgasm after orgasm, I had the strangest feeling that we were drifting further and further apart and that there was nothing that I could do to stop it. Afterward, we lay together, wrapped in each other's arms until we fell asleep while all thoughts of dinner were cast aside.

Shattered Dreams

The next day I spent time with my mother and the rest of my friends, and I did not see Davis until the following day when he came to drive me to the airport. We drove in silence and I could tell that he was thinking deeply about everything that had happened. When he dropped me off at the gate, he said he would write me and that we were still okay but somehow it just did not ring true. I boarded my plane with a heavy heart and dozed off on the plane until I arrived back in Texas.

Terry and Kat picked me up from the airport and I poured out my heart to them telling them about the beautiful proposal, the ring, the rest stop where I lost the ring, and how heartbroken both Davis and I were over the loss of the ring. I told them that although Davis says that he still loves me and misses me I could not help but feel that we will not be getting married any time soon and probably will not be together for much longer either.

Terry turned me toward her with both hands on my shoulders and gently shook me saying, "Stop it right now. I don't believe that it is over for you two – just look at me and Timothy. We have been through a lot together, good, and bad but we are still holding onto each other."

Kat smiled pulling us both in for a group hug and said, "Now that's what I'm talking about – positive thinking. Just give him some time and just wait and see – he will call and reassure you."

Terry and Kat tried their best to reassure me that losing the ring does not mean the end of our relationship, but I know what I felt in my heart and that was that I had lost my soulmate back in that restroom on the way back to Philly. I felt that Davis would never see me the same way again – ever. I did not feel much like hanging out, so Terry and Kat dropped me off at my place, and then they went home as well.

As life on base continued with Keith no longer there to bother me, days turned into weeks and then turned into months. The letters from Davis were slowing down and on one of his last letters, I received the answer that I dreaded most of all. Scanning the letter quickly, past all the hopes that I was well, comments that he is well and so is Auntie, I suddenly see the words "former girlfriend, Jasmin" and I freeze.

Tears start falling and I angrily thrust the letter aside. I didn't, couldn't read anymore because I could almost see him standing in front of me saying, 'we are just handing out right now, nothing serious. I just want to be honest with you and tell you everything that's going on in my life right now.'

My chest was so tight that I started hyperventilating and I had to force myself to breathe slowly. I jumped up from the bed and began to look frantically for the letter. I had so angrily cast aside moments ago. Leaning over the left side of my bunk, I spied the bawled-up letter in the corner between the bed post and the wall. Still crying, wiping tears from my eyes, I read the rest of the letter. We were over. Although Davis didn't say those words that's what I felt.

I did not call him, and I also could not bring myself to write back because I did not know what to say to him that could change his mind about us. I decided to just focus on my job and life on base and for the time being, but all thought of us aside until I could figure out what to say. I was trying desperately to hold onto the notion that Davis and I were soulmates.

Many nights I fell asleep with images of our family, house, and life as husband and wife swirling around in my head. Davis would have a job at Conrail as a train conductor and I would either just be a homemaker like Auntie or work part-time at the bank while raising our children. We would spend the summers going back and forth to Baltimore to spend time with his cousins, Tammy, Felicia, Beth, and their children.

As it was, I had spent so much time with them that I already felt like I was a part of the family. That's what I daydreamed about most of the time on base. Those thoughts gave me hope that somehow, someway Davis and I would find ourselves back together again.

The Ill-Fated Invitation

The summer seemed to pass by quickly, and suddenly it was late August, and everyone was getting ready for our Labor Day break. Terry was taking time off to fly back home to Chicago and introduce her fiancé to her family. Kat was also flying back home to New York to see her family as well while I decided to stay on base. Well, I did not so much as decide as my lack of funds pretty much decided for me that I would not be flying anywhere for Labor Day break.

Totally without realizing it, I began to change the way I handled stressful situations. Feeling as if Davis and I were no more and having gone through what I went through with SSgt Davis, I began to compartmentalize my feelings. I put painful memories and experiences into perfect little boxes, storing them away so that I could function and perform my duties to the best of my ability. This technique seemed to work well for me along with going out to the NCO club every chance I got to relax over a couple of drinks.

Tequila was my drink of choice by this time. I also had developed a unique fondness for downing anywhere from 3 to 5 boilermakers at a time whenever I as out with my girls. Most people consumed their boilermakers with a shot of whiskey dropped into a glass half-filled with beer while I chose to drink mine with a shot of Jose Cuervo-while not gold. Whenever thoughts and memories threatened to creep up into the present, I quickly found ways to distract myself by doing other things mostly because drinking was legal and easy to come by in Abilene, Texas. Drinking and honing my skills as a master compartmentalizer gave me space to breathe and feel normal around other people.

One day, TSgt Alameda invited me out with my fellow airmen to his house for the Labor Day barbecue. I knew that the male airmen gathered together over the TSgt Alameda's house at least once a month or so to have eaten and relax, but I had never been invited before, so this felt nice, like I would finally be looked upon as 'one of the guys' and not like some stuck-up airman that got the cushy job in dispatch. I had heard on the grapevine that a few of my fellow airmen were not happy that I got that job, and they felt like I only got the job because I was a female and not because I was qualified as that position was typically only given to E-4's and above and here I was a lowly E-2.

It was not until many years later that I wondered if segregating female airman and giving them a position of leadership within the unit was simply TSgt Alameda's way of ingratiating himself to female airman as a way of gaining their trust. And it worked because I let my guard down around him. After everything that I had already been through, I felt a strong need to belong to the group, to be accepted as just another one of the guys. I knew that not all the guys saw me as a threat because some of them were of the same rank as me and they were new to Dyess AFB as well. As a result, they hadn't had any more time than me to make friends and cultivate alliances.

Brushing off their resentment, I accepted the invitation feeling good about attending the barbecue because it would be an opportunity for everyone to relax and maybe get to know one another better. I didn't know much about them and they didn't know much about me, so we were all even-steven.

The day of the barbecue arrived, and it was a nice, sunny day with a gentle breeze blowing. Everyone had gathered around in TSgt Alameda's backyard smoking cigarettes, drinking beers, and joking around. After a while, someone suggested that we play Cardinal Puff-Puff and TSgt

Alameda brought out the booze and we started playing. It seemed like a fun game and no one seemed to be hesitant to play so I thought it was ok for me to indulge as well, after all, how else were we going to get to know one another better?

TSgt Alameda was a generous host and he set out an array of liquor, including tequila, rum and vodka. As I mentioned earlier, Cardinal Puff-Puff is a drinking game which basically involved making a series of movements as you give honor to Cardinal Puff-Puff. Each time you mess up the words or the movements you are forced to down a shot of liquor. It is a high-spirited and inane game and by the time you get into it good everyone laughs hysterically when someone forgets the movements and is made to down a shot of liquor. It is a given that all participants may end up very drunk, and it is not unusual for players to also pass out from consumption.

I was able to maintain a semblance of sobriety at times during the game, but on this day, I was genuinely enjoying letting go and being silly with my fellow airmen. I was drinking Tequila and the others were drinking rum, vodka and any other hard liquor that could be found in his house. We all had each other's backs and if we got tipsy—well then that was the point.

Of course, I lost the game becoming totally drunk at which time TSgt Alameda suggested that I go lie down for a while until I could get myself together. He took me inside and laid me down on a bed and before I knew it, I had passed out. Even though I was more than a little drunk, I felt completely at ease around my fellow airman. There was no reason for fear or apprehension because everyone seemed to be getting just as drunk as I was, and I knew by the time I woke up that I would naturally find everyone else had passed out and taken a nap as well.

Light Blue Curtains

I don't know how long I was passed out, but I came to only to find TSgt Alameda on top of me, fumbling with my pants, and my shirt was pushed up to my chest. As I struggled to become fully awake and tried to get out of from under him (to no avail) I realized that he was suddenly inside me. I continued to struggle to get from under him, but he was too heavy. He was saying something in my ear and telling me to be quiet.

I was frozen and didn't know what to do as I struggled to become fully awake and move him off me. I tried turning my body, but every time I tried to turn, I found his arm blocking my movements. I began to cry and turned to look out the window to see if someone could come to help me, and my eyes landed on Harrison, who was staring right through the window, and it seemed to me that he could see right through me.

Harrison was a tall, lanky dude whose uniform never seemed to fit him well he also couldn't see very well and as a result wore some heavy, thick-rimmed glasses. We all used to have a laugh together talking about the terrible eyeglasses they give you to wear in the air force and often would try on each other's glasses just to see whose eyes were the worst. Harrison always won because he had the worst sight of anyone in our unit. Harrison, however, did have some of the most piercing blue eyes that I had ever seen on a white man before, and when you contrast that with his jet-black hair and thin mustache, he wasn't a bad-looking dude. Of course, he had no muscles underneath his uniform so for the most part that's why his uniform never seemed to fit him well. He always looked as if he had on someone else's uniform.

Harrison had a cup in his right hand and was raising his cup to his face to take a sip, I guess, and he was laughing at something that someone had said at the same time.

I saw his face clearly through the sheer light blue curtains and I moved my lips to say something, but no sound came out. I heard them laughing outside the window and just as quickly as I noticed Harrison staring at me, he turned his back to the window and kept laughing with the other guys. Did he see me, or did he only see the darkness behind the curtain? Most likely due to his bad eyesight, Harrison did not see me at all and that was to my misfortune.

I laid there for seemingly hours but was more like minutes as TSgt Alameda kept humping and humping away at me like I was just a sponge with no backbone and no shape whatsoever. At some point, I blacked out again, and the next thing I knew I was back in my room on the base, having no recollection as to how I'd gotten there. Hyper-encoding is fully enforced and activated.

I was raped by my immediate commander at the age of 20 while serving in the United States Air Force. Here my mother thought she was saving me from the certain doom of becoming impregnated at the age of 15 and going on to live a humdrum life as a teenage unwed mother, and instead, I had been attacked and violated not once, but twice while serving my country. I learned the hard way that it does no good to file a complaint, so needless to say, I did not file a complaint against my TSgt Alameda. I honestly couldn't think of what to do, so, I did nothing.

No More Sleazeballs In My Life... Please!

When I say I did nothing I mean I did absolutely nothing. I reported to duty but couldn't stand working in dispatch anymore. SSgt Brown began to pick on me coming up to me while on duty and whispering in my ear "Hey, Green, can I get some?" with a wicked and sickening grin on his face.

I can only guess that TSgt Alameda had told him something because I didn't say a word obviously. It was very difficult for me to continue working in dispatch and out of nowhere suddenly I didn't have to work dispatch anymore. TSgt Alameda had pulled me from that post, put Harrison in my place, and put me back on patrol duty. I can only guess that he couldn't figure out what to do with me and maybe he was afraid of what I would say or do.

It is difficult to overstate how seriously I misjudged the character of my fellow airmen and the extent to which I believed that I was safe among my fellow airmen at a backyard barbecue. As I downed glass after glass with the others, I felt I was finally getting a chance that day to forgive myself-for losing the ring of the man I loved so truly, for leaving home at all, for ending up so far away from my beloved mother, the comfort of my old neighborhood and for leaving the friends I had known all my life.

Yes, I was headed out on an adventure and it meant leaving all that I loved behind, but since Mama Ruth always had my best interest at heart, and since we were both in agreement about my enlistment, nothing could go wrong. Absolutely nothing could go wrong, right?

I COUNT THE DARK

How I wish that there had been huge red flags, alarm bells, anything, something that would have told me to be less trusting of those people who somehow, I seemed to place my trust in so completely. When you enlist and go through basic training you delete all mention of the word 'I' and you learn that everyone becomes a 'we' as we learn to work as a unit. Transitioning from basic training to my permanent duty station was an acknowledgement that now I belonged to a unit, a part of a team, something bigger than myself. Naturally, I trusted my peers because we were all on the same team – or so I thought at the time all of 20 years old, and on my own in the Air Force.

Terry and Kat came back from Labor Day weekend all bubbly and cheerful telling me about their vacations. Terry told me that "Everybody in her family just loved Timothy" and Kat said, she started back dating a guy she knew from high school during her break, so she had a really good time back in New York." I couldn't tell them what happened. I was still in shock and numb from the experience, so I did my best to act like everything was normal. They soon found out that I was no longer acting dispatcher and wondered how I felt about it. I lied and said I was totally ok with it and they seemed to accept my decision. I awoke one morning to being called down to see TSgt Alameda. The way he acted you would never have thought that he raped me. He carried on as if nothing was different. It was as if I didn't exist and that I was just another faceless airman assigned to his unit.

I didn't know why he requested to see me especially since he did his best to avoid me every shift but as soon as I arrived in his office, I could tell that something was going to be different about this visit. Little did I know that my life as I knew it was about to become even harder. I was totally unprepared for what happened next. TSgt Alameda informed me, "Airman Green, we received word from home that your father has died. You are to report home immediately to attend the funeral services and report back to base afterward. You will be given five days leave to attend to your affairs. The Red Cross is at your disposal to help you make the flight arrangements.

Dismissed.

I almost crumbled right there in front of him, but somehow, I held my composure and stood at parade rest until he finished giving me orders.

By the time I made it back to my room, Terry and Kat were there having already heard (somehow) that I would be going home to attend my father's funeral. They both helped me pack and held me as I cried and tried to get myself together. I left for home and can only tell you that the experience was the most surreal experience of my life. I felt as if I were sleepwalking and not even present during the entire time I was home. Davis was there to help me settle in, but I honestly cannot even recall what we talked about, where we hung out, or even what I wore to my father's funeral. Before I knew it, the services were over, and I was on the plane heading back to Dyess AFB.

As I sat in my window sweat, aisle number 22, I found myself drifting off to sleep with thoughts of my father in my head. I remembered the time he took me to the hospital to get my leg stitched up and another time we rode in his car to go get water ice. I struggled to remember other meaningful moments like the time he took us all to Coney Island and Wildwood, New Jersey. Falling asleep I began to have a clearer picture of my dad and I realized that we never really spent much time together while I was growing up. Honestly, my father's death and my experiences attending his funeral were all a blur to me to this day. Hyper-encoding once again to the rescue.

All I seem to remember about the funeral was Mama and my siblings getting dressed in all black. Being driven in my father's friend Mr. Jones's car and how I didn't even register what the feel of his hand on my knee, squeezing it meant at the moment. I remember being frozen as his hand moved up my thigh and staring at the emblem on the dashboard as I felt my body lifting, floating up to the roof of his car. Just as quickly as he laid his hand on my thigh, he removed his hand as if it was never there, and then we were at Powell Funeral home. Lots of people gathered inside and again all I heard were different voices moving all around me.

At some point, I realized that I was sitting down and lots of different people were speaking about my dad. I thought back to the last time that I had seen him and how small he appeared to be as he leaned on his crutches revealing his right leg bandaged at the thigh, because they had to cut it off to stop the gangrene from moving all throughout his body. At 6 ft. 2, my father, Erroll Rutherford Wilson, nicknamed 'Money' because he was always giving it out, seemed like a shell of a man. As I stared at him the acrid smell of his unfiltered Camel cigarettes stung my nostrils, so I had to close and blink my eyes several times to clear the smoke away.

Pulling myself back into the present, I noticed that the service was over and everyone was trying to figure out who was riding home back to Marston street for the wake. Somehow, I wound up in my stepbrother Rusty's car just riding and riding. Rusty was talking about something and I could hear myself responding but I don't know what I said. Before I knew it, Rusty had taken me to the Inntowner Motor Lodge, and he was kissing me before the door closed. I know that we had sex because my panties were wet after I had gotten dressed and he had dropped me back off on Marston Street. Did I imagine Mr. Jones had on my thigh? Did Rusty rape me as well or did I consent? To this day, I have no memory except for these traumatic flashes, flashes of being violated, of being touched and handled without my consent. It was as if I had no awareness of my body at all, if I had no will and no ability to stop these intrusions, as if I was frozen in horror, and both my psyche and body vacated the premises. All of this is confusing and till a blur to me many years later. Hyper-encoding again.

James Wilson Green aka "Slim"

After a couple of months of what seemed like normalcy, my world was rocked again by the death of my older brother James exactly 30 days after my father. Once again, the Red Cross came to my rescue and I was ever so grateful for their financial support because I had no money at all for plane fares. My brother James committed suicide, and his death devastated my mother the most and my older brothers Little Junior and Jason.

I found out years later that the reason my brother, Little Junior, was hospitalized after my brother James's death was that he had run all the way from our home in the Wynnefield section of the city to North Philadelphia, which is a very long distance if you know the streets of Philadelphia, to my brother James' house on the 3100 block of Marston Street and busts down the door before the police or paramedics arrived and tried to cut my brother down from where his body was hanging. He was standing there trying to hold him up when the paramedics arrived. As a result, my brother, psyche snapped, and he was diagnosed with Manic-Depressive, Bipolar disorder.

I can only imagine what an image that must have been when the paramedics arrived to see my brother struggling to hold onto my older brother to loosen the noose around his neck in an attempt to stop him from suffocating, but according to all reports that I heard, by the time my brother, Little Junior had arrived at James' house, my brother, James, was already dead. My mother's world all but shattered as the reality that she had lost the love of her life and her second-born son all in less than a few short months. My beautiful, strong mother, who had stopped smoking her Saratoga 120's

Menthol, in the green pack and her Benson and Hedges, menthol, once again turned back to smoking in addition to upping her daily intake of gin to help smooth out the edges around her grief. It was this pattern of self-medicating grief that would ultimately lead to her death years later from breast cancer which then also spread to her lungs.

My brother James, nickname Slick, was a very funny, yet serious dude who could sew his ass off. His tailor-made slacks, coats, vests, and shirts were in high demand on the streets of North Philly. His best friend, Mac, aka Kevin Waters, and he were friends ever since junior high school and they held fashion shows in my Mom's living room and anywhere else they could find a spot. My brother had survived Vietnam and found a way to turn his life around after many, many struggles he had when he first returned from Vietnam. My brother could be sweet as cotton candy one minute and then as angry as a hornet nest the next. For years, I never knew there was something wrong with him as a result of being sprayed with Agent Orange in Vietnam, I just assumed that he was exuding normal behavior. At one time he worked as a teacher's aide or something like that at the Greentree School where my brother Jason attended for a short time, although he and Jason were not there at the same time.

Little Junior and Jason both looked up to our brothers James and Jackson because they had heard stories about how crazy stuff went down over there in Vietnam. My brother Jackson enlisted in the Airforce first and then later my brother James followed him in going to the Marines. Although I was a young kid, I can still remember seeing my mother sitting on the steps waiting on the mailman to come hoping she would receive a letter from one of my brothers. She would read parts of their letters to us and save special parts for herself to read in private. Most of the time I liked my brother James because he had one of the brightest smiles, twinkling eyes, and the most infectious laugh of everyone in the family.

He was also very smart and good with math with his left-handed self. He could draw, paint, sew, dance, write poetry and tell jokes making everyone laugh. If you were to ask me if there was anything that my brother James couldn't do, I would have told you nope – he can do anything he sets his mind to. As a little girl and then later as a teenager, the only thing that I saw which caused me to look at him somewhat differently was how his temper could come out of nowhere and how he seemed to run in between two girlfriends, Ms. Nancy, mother of my niece Daisy and Ms. Jennifer, mother of my niece Tammy. One minute he was with Ms. Nancy and the next I knew he was with Ms. Jennifer. It wasn't up to me to figure out the dynamics of their relationship, so I left it alone.

All these memories of my brothers James, Jackson, Little Junior, and Jason came rushing back to me with the news of my brother James' passing. We may not have been as close as siblings should be, mainly due to our age gap, but I still loved all of my brothers fiercely yet differently.

Once again, I drifted thru another funeral barely able to remember who said what, when, why, and where it all happened at all. I know that I was present because I can remember Davis being by my side but honestly, we were no longer seeing each other so I do not know why he came to the funeral other than just to see me and out of respect for my family. For the most part, I think he just stayed by my side and let me lean on him for support for old times' sake.

Detachment

By the time the funeral was over, and I had returned to base, I could feel that I was even more different, detached than when I left. The things that were fun to do were no longer as much fun. Terry stopped by my room several times trying to get me to go off base with her to party and I begged off time and time again with excuses that she knew were bogus but because she was my friend, she pretty much just let it go after a while. I began to stay on base more during my three-day breaks and distanced myself from my friends.

Kat also tried to get me to go to the NCO club several times, but I gave her some of the same excuses I gave Terry, and she left me alone as well. There was one time when both Terry and Kat decided to double-team me and started crazy knocking on my door one Friday night, and they dragged me out to the NCO club just to get me out of my room. I hung out with them for the night just because I knew they weren't going to take no for an answer that night. I sat at the bar most of the night, just sipping on one tequila sunrise the entire night. I never got up to dance at all, I just sat until it was closing time, and then we all went back to the barracks.

It felt like my world had ended as if I was a speck of dust blown by the wind in every direction possible. I left home and Davis and wound up more than a thousand miles away in Abilene, Texas, STOP. I became a Desk Sergeant (pseudo) and my fellow airmen hated me for it, STOP! I was assaulted by SSgt Davis and nothing changed on base, STOP! I was raped by TSgt Alameda. STOP! I was too scared to report it because they did not do anything about SSgt Davis and he was of a lower rank than my TSgt, so why bother, STOP! My father died STOP! My brother died STOP! I was screaming at the top of my lungs to the entire world STOP! STOP! STOP! They did not know that I was the little girl from the 2400 block of Marston street who many older adults called little Tina 'Turner' Green because I could be found singing my head off all the time to the beat of Tina Turner's "Proud Mary" and Natalie Cole's "This Will Be" (An Everlasting Love). But as hard as I tried, I could not make anything stop. I was nothing but a big mess with no hope of a happy ending in sight.

No! Not again!
I was a zombie as I walked around base during that time, reporting to duty day after day with no real purpose in mind. Out of the blue, Sgt. Berlmont started trying to chat me up and we met off and on at the base club to share a drink or two. He was 5' 9" with dark chocolate skin and some serious pearly whites. He had light brown eyes and a small scar just under his left eye. He wanted to date me, but I didn't want to date him at all and at this time I was still confused about what was happening with Davis and me anyway. I had made a mental note to just take things easy for a while and stay away from any and all relationships with men. My judgment was way off since the whole incident with SSgt. Davis, TSgt Alameda, Sleazeball Jones, Rusty, heck, ALL MEN IN GENERAL! I no longer felt like I couldn't trust myself to make the right choices anymore where men were concerned.

One day as I was on my way back from lunch when Sgt. Berlmont grabbed me and pulled me into the stairwell and started plying me with questions. He wanted to know, "What is wrong with me? Why won't you date me?" He had heard about me and Keith Davis and wanted to know what was so good about Keith Davis that was better than him?

I told him, "I really don't feel like talking right now."

I tried to step around him to take the stairs and go to my room but he wouldn't move out of my way. In my mind, I'm wondering what has gotten into him. The other night it seemed like he took the brush off well, yet now here he was behaving like such a brute. I started to feel afraid, thoughts started rushing into my brain of SSgt. Davis, TSgt Almeda, my father, my father's friend, Rusty, my brother's death, and now this dude in my face. I was angry but before I could raise my voice and give him a piece of my mind, he suddenly grabbed me by the collar and proceeded to drag me up the steps on my back to his floor. I struggled to remain upright and tried to turn around so that my back and butt weren't bouncing up and down the stairs, but I couldn't get a grip. I was yelling at him to stop and let me go but he wouldn't listen.

In a flash, we were at the top of the landing and the door opened inward. Berlmont saw the other airman coming into the stairwell and suddenly let me go and ran inside, I presume to his room. The guy helped me up to my feet and down to my floor because my back was hurt, and I just knew that I was going to be sore and scratched up from his attack. I couldn't believe that once again I was the victim of a stupid attack by a dumb ass Sgt. that couldn't figure out how to take 'NO' as an answer.

This attack made me feel different somehow. In a weird way, it broke me out of my depression somewhat because suddenly I realized how angry I was at all men in general and specifically SSgt Davis, TSgt Almeda, and now Sgt Berlmont! Back in my room my mind was still reeling over what had happened. What was wrong with these men was that they all felt like they could treat me any way they wanted to and get away with it! I mean here we are, two black people in the Airforce, one female and one male. I expected to be treated better by the black people in the military than the white people yet here I was victimized yet again. I had heard stories of other female airmen being mistreated by their male counterparts, but it seemed like most of those stories were not about black women.

No one was walking around base at that time telling stories of being raped or sexually assaulted in the military. Back then, these were the first inklings of what I know for sure today: I was dealing with a culture of hierarchy, masculinity, and power as old as time. I had grown up at a time when Westerns were still popular on television and women were portrayed as damsels in distress who needed a man to come along and make things right for them on the ranch. Images of women in media usually showed them playing subservient roles. And rarely did we see an image of a woman in the military being depicted in a position of authority. Positions of authority in the military at that time were mostly held by men, and no matter the rank, the man's word was always taken over women. I am almost certain that if any women were to have spoken up back then in the late 70's that they were most likely spoken to by a superior and told to just forget all about it and let it go because nothing good will come of it.

Dyess AFB-The End

As a member of law enforcement stationed at Dyess Air Force Base in Abilene, Texas, I do not recall ever responding to a call from base housing related to sexual assault, although I do recall responding to a couple of domestic situations. In those instances, the calls did not turn out to be sexual assault incidents but were rather spousal arguments that seemed to get out of hand.

As I reflected on Sgt. Berlmont and my assault in the stairwell, my thoughts ran to thoughts of my mom, but I didn't run to the phone to call her because I knew she was still going through it due to the deaths of my father and brother. It was at this time that I began to believe that all military men seemed to think they were entitled to behave any way they wanted without fear of reprisal when it came to me. I do not know what the statistics were at the time regarding military sexual assault or even if the term was ever bounced around at that time, but I knew that from my experiences, the military did not seem to value my word over another airman. Yet, still, I promised myself that I would file a complaint this time because my body was aching, I had bruises, and surely, they must believe me this time. I somehow fell asleep and didn't wake up until the next morning, feeling so thankful I had off the next day because I was really sore.

Did I Hear Someone Say... Complaint?

I complained and was once again told that Sgt Berlmont would be questioned and, if necessary, an investigation would be conducted. I just assumed that everything would turn out well because, this time, there was a witness, and I had bruises. I knew there just had to be some punishment coming Sgt Berlmont's way for hurting me, and after all, there was a witness. He may not have seen everything that happened, but he knew something wasn't right when he stepped into that stairwell.

As I continued to report to duty for my next nine-day shift about midway thru my shift I received another call to report to my immediate commander TSgt Alameda and was told that my grandmother had suffered a medical emergency and they didn't think that she would make it. At this point, it was only a few months since both my father and my brother had died so I could only imagine what my mother must be going through back home. I was told that I could take leave again if I felt that I had to, or I could just stay on base and wait to see what happened. I decided to stay on base because I didn't have that much time saved up and I didn't know if my grandmother was going to pass or not so just in case, I needed to take the time later I would have it available to take.

Well, thankfully, my grandmother pulled through and I didn't need to take any more time off to go back to Philly. However, not all was well at Dyess AFB because after a short few weeks, I received a request to report to the base commander's office yet again where I learned that they were not going to proceed with an investigation. I was informed that Sgt Berlmont stated we were boyfriend and girlfriend; we had an argument and things got physical. Sgt Berlmont reported that I scratched him and that he pushed me and then quickly grabbed me to keep me from falling and that this is what the other airman saw when he entered the stairwell. As a result, there would be no charges filed. Also, Sgt. Berlmonts' orders came thru, and he has been shipped out to his Base of Preference which explains why I no longer saw him hanging around my barracks for the last week.

To say that I was stunned is an understatement. I was really angry this time, but I couldn't think of what I could do to resolve this issue. Was there no recourse for me anywhere? No redress for the abuse that I suffered from SSgt Davis, TSgt Alameda, and now Sgt. Berlmont? I was made to feel as if female airmen were never to be taken at their word and that a man could simply say anything to another man about a 'he-said, she-said' event and his word would always be believed over hers. As if I weren't serving in our nation's military but instead was engaged in a series of lovers' quarrels! The fact that the base commander really took it on faith that Sgt. Berlmont was telling the truth and that therefore, I must have been lying was an acknowledgment of the patriarchal nature of the military and how little credence was given to women in the military during that time. We simply were not believed, and in many ways, this way of undermining women and questioning the validity of the acts of violence and abuse we've endured continues today.

I had already complained to the highest-ranking person on base so there was nothing else to do but be grateful that Berlmont would no longer be around to harass me. Twice-attacked with no resolutions in sight, and I had suffered through the loss of my father and brother and almost my grandmother – this man's Airforce was not turning out to be what I had thought it would be.

The ability to successfully compartmentalize some of the most painful experiences that we go through in life is critical to being able to wake up every morning and be a functioning member of society. Compartmentalization was always my go-to in moments of severe stress and anxiety. That ability allowed some semblance of normalcy to return for me on base. I began to feel a little of the emptiness over the loss of my father and brother that had never really resolved itself. I pretty much just put all my thoughts of them out of my mind and focused really hard on work. I worked hard on duty and began to party a little bit more with my friends.

As the days turned into weeks, a sudden depression came over me and I began to feel the weight of my father's and brothers' deaths, which caused me to feel like a walking zombie. Additionally, the realization that I had been raped and the fact that I couldn't tell anyone kept running on a loop in my head as well. I don't know how I went to work every day or how the days flew by one after the other because I was in a daze most of the time. I felt sad all the time and after work, I just took to staying in my room. Kat and Terry would come by to try to convince me to go out with them, but I would beg off and just tell them that I did not feel up to it and lie and say it was because of my father or brother's death but in reality, it was the rape that was holding me down most of all.

I couldn't find any way to numb the pain that I was feeling and continuing to work and act as if nothing was wrong took its toll on me. One evening I decided to end it all. I looked in my medicine cabinet and found some cold tablets, vitamins, aspirin, and some pills I didn't recognize and just downed them all with some cherry Kool-Aid. I wanted to just sleep the pain away and after a while, I began to fall asleep. At some point during that night, I remember throwing up and I remember Terry and Kat were with me trying to help me stay awake. They helped me to the bathroom and helped me to throw up some more pills and wiped the sweat off my forehead. I was shaking, groggy, and felt totally weak. Terry told me that everything would be okay and shared with me about the time her grandmother died. She said it was the worst kind of pain anyone could feel, so she could only imagine how I must be feeling having lost both my father and brother so close together. Kat didn't say too much, opting to just remain quiet and hold my hand and rub my shoulders every so often.

No one said the words "suicide attempt" aloud the whole night but they both knew what I had tried to do and they both seemed genuinely glad that I had not succeeded. They stayed with me all night long just to watch over me and didn't leave my side until the next day when they had to go to work. I just happened to be on my 3-day break so there was nowhere that I wanted or needed to go and I mostly stayed in my room. I remember standing in the bathroom hours later looking at my eyes and noticing how dilated my pupils were and wondering why I wasn't dead.

As the days went by, I started to shut down even more and it was hard to report to duty on a daily basis. I remember having a conversation with another sergeant on my shift about how I was feeling sad, alone, and depressed. He had somehow heard about the incidents with SSgt Davis and Sgt Berlmont but did not know about TSgt Alameda so he knew that that coupled with the deaths of my father and brother were weighing on my mind. He told me that if I thought that the military was no longer the place for me and that I want to go home right now, all I needed to do was report to duty, go to the armory to have my weapon assigned and then march to the middle of the room and simply say these words: "I feel like shooting something tonight." He told me that once I utter those words, I will be stripped of my weapon so fast that it would make my head spin. I thought about it over a few more days of my 9-day shift and then one night while I was in the armory I mentioned to another sergeant, Sgt Melvin, that I felt like I was going to shoot something tonight and as predicted, all hell broke loose. Before I could blink, I was stripped of my weapon and told to report to my barracks. I was excused from duty until further notice.

After a few days, I was told to report to the base shrink for an evaluation. I reported for my evaluation and told the psychiatrist that I no longer felt safe around weapons; I said that I felt like one day I might shoot myself or someone else. In reality, I only said those things because I felt at the time that the USAF was no longer the place for me, I wanted out because of all that had happened to me and because my sergeant told me that if I just "acted crazy" they would discharge me. I never spoke about being attacked because, at this point, I no longer felt like I could trust anyone on base to handle any of my concerns. I was told to return to my barracks until a final report was prepared. The report instructed me to report to duty at a different unit where I wouldn't have to carry a weapon. Shortly after the report came back, I was up for leave so I didn't report to my new unit right away and instead went home to Philly for a week to clear my head.

At home, my frozen exterior just melted away once I was back in my mother's presence. One day my mother and I were sitting in her bedroom and she was focused on her crossword puzzle book intently while I was laying across her bed glancing through a magazine. Mama-dear had on her house coat with her bare feet just hanging off the bed. Her readers were perched so precariously on the bridge of her nose that it seemed like they would fall off with the slightest movement. It was a pretty sunny day and I had on a loose top and a pair of jeans. Mama-dear paused and looked up from her crossword puzzle and stared intently at me, she opened her mouth slightly saying 'Are you ok? Are you ready to go back? You just seem so content to be here and you are almost acting as if you don't want to go back'. My back stiffened just a little as mama spoke and I tried to roll over and look at her since I was just lying on my stomach, but I couldn't move. Soft quiet tears began streaming down my face and before I knew it, I was crying full blast and Mama-Ruth just leaned over and pulled me into her arms saying… All right…all right… let it out, baby. Finding my voice, I sighed and began telling her everything that had happened to me on base.

Mama would mostly hold me in her arms but every few seconds or so, she would straighten up and begin cursing. She started with "What the hell!" and went straight to "That's some bull" and 'Hell NO! We are going to get this straightened out!"

We sat like that for a while, with me talking and mama cussing and wiping my tears away. She held me so gently and rocked me to sleep just like I was a little baby. The next day mama walked into my room, turned on the light, tilted her head to the side, and said, "Get up and come on downstairs so we can talk about this some more."

I pushed back the covers and sat up. "Yes ma'am, I'll be right down."

When I got downstairs Mama was sitting at the dining room table having her usual, a cup of hot black tea, no sugar, and a slice of plain melba toast with half of red grapefruit. Looking up and then standing up, she looked at me, "Do you want some tea? There's some hot water left on the stove."

I pulled up a chair and sat down. "No, I'm good."

Mama started strong, "When you return to base you are going to go straight to your—what do you call him?—base commander's office and demand to see him to report being raped. Also, tell him about being removed from your post and being transferred to another unit. He will have to hear you out. Aren't they told to listen to you in these situations?

I shook my head. "Honestly, I don't know much about what they are told. All I know is that it's hard to get a meeting with him and once I tell them what it's about it will probably be doubly hard to get in there but I'm going to try."

She stood up, came around to me, took my chin in her hand, and lifted up my face. "You are going to do more than try, you are going to just do it."

Article 15-UCMJ

Naturally, I tried to do what my mama said but as soon as I got back to base, I was put under arrest. I was informed that I was excused from duty, charged with failure to report to duty and that Article 15 procedures would be filed against me. Apparently, I had misread my orders and as it turns out I was supposed to have reported back to duty earlier and when I failed to report to duty, they started filing charges against me. I was so out of it while home on leave that I misread my return date and didn't get back to base on time. At home, I felt safe and warm. I had my mother beside me, which helped me feel stronger, but I did not want to go back to base, so I must have subconsciously stayed behind an extra day. Dyess AFB and all the ugliness that happened there was the furthest thing from my mind, and I found any excuse I could to stay in Philadelphia.

I requested to see the base commander again, but my request was denied, and I was remanded to my quarters. While I was in my room, I was denied visitors so there was no way for me to communicate anything to anyone.

After a few days, I was allowed a hearing to determine if Article 15 procedures should continue moving forward. At my hearing, the only information allowed to be discussed was the pending charges. I tried to explain what happened and why, but it was all to no avail because from the military's perspective there was no denying the fact that I had failed to report to duty.

In a matter of days, I was stripped of my AIC rank, my base pay was reduced, and I was forced to remain in my barracks again until a final disposition of my case and punishment had been decided. I was told that if I agreed to the reduction in rank and returned to duty as an Airman that the proceedings would stop and that I could return to work and begin my career all over again.

At this point, I could no longer embrace the USAF as a way of life for me. All I could think about was being attacked by SSgt Davis and told there were no grounds for an investigation; then being raped by TSgt Alameda, and then being attacked and physically dragged up two flights of stairs by Sgt Berlmont, which was reconfigured as a spat between girlfriend and boyfriend that didn't merit investigation. Thoughts of being home permanently in North Philadelphia suddenly looked like the safest place in the world for me so I disagreed with their recommendation and decided to take my punishment. I informed my unit commander that I was not going to report back to work so the Air Force began following through with paperwork to discharge me from service.

Everything that was happening to me was totally crazy. Before I was attacked, all of my earlier experiences on base seemed very normal. The main form of relaxation on base involved hanging out at the NCO club, drinking, and dancing the night away. Alcohol was the primary game in town if you wanted to take the edge off after work to de-stress. The only way to 'fit-in' was to drink, which meant participating in drinking games like Cardinal Puff-Puff. I did what everyone else was doing to have a good time. Before joining the military, I was neither a drinker nor a smoker. Heck, I can still remember being kicked off an entire theatre production, "Why Do We Need A Title," at Freedom Theatre when a bunch of us were caught sharing a cigarette between shows. Overall, I was just another invisible black female on base trying to be a part of the team.

I was the one who had been violated, yet I was the only one up on charges and about to go before a panel that would decide my fate in the military. Where were the perpetrators in all of this? Out enjoying the rest of their life in the military and stationed at their base of preference to boot! This was the epitome of irony in my eyes, me sitting around awaiting my fate and those sergeants enjoying their time in other locations with no one the wiser about what they had done to me. The guilty are very rarely punished as far as I could see.

In less than two weeks I was sitting before the base commander again being told that I was being recommended for a general discharge under honorable conditions and that as a result of this type of a discharge I would retain my GI Bill benefits, which included education and the ability to obtain a home mortgage somewhere down the road in life.

Military Discharge

"The most beautiful people I've known are those who have known trials, have known struggles, have known loss, and have found their way out of the depths."
– Elizabeth Kübler-Ross

During my discharge, the furthest thing from my mind was an acknowledgment of the future benefits that I could one day receive because of my service to my country. I enlisted with the hope of serving this great country to the best of my ability, and instead I was subjected to mental abuse, physical attacks, and rape by my superior who only saw me as a body to be picked apart and not as a fellow airman to be respected.

I was released from the USAF in February 1981 after almost two years of service. I returned home to Philadelphia to a much different lifestyle because of my experiences. I grew so much during the two years that I spent away from home. I entered the United States Air Force as a naïve teenager eager to see the world and learn new things and returned to Philadelphia as a young woman whose eyes were now wide open to the abuse that women are subjected to at the hands of men.

Originally, my job in the Air Force was to be a radio dispatch operator stationed at Minot Air Force Base in North Dakota, but because life became more stressful due to the number of gang wars happening all around me in North Philly, my mother and I decided to forego my BOP and my guaranteed job and simply take whatever job and base designation that the Air Force had available for me at the time.

I think back to how I wound up at Dyess AFB as a Law Enforcement officer, and I find myself wondering how different my life would have been if I had just stuck it out and waited the extra three months to be placed in a guaranteed job. Would my life have turned out differently? Would I still be enlisted in the Air Force? I felt that if I had waited the extra three months that my career in the Air force would have turned out much differently. For starters, I would have met a different caliber of airmen and officers. I imagined that most of them would have been studious types like me and serious-minded, focused solely on their careers and performing their duties to the best of their abilities. I would have set my sights on marrying an officer and going to school to complete my degree so that I could attain the officer's rank one day as well.

If I had remained as enlisted personnel, I would have strived for E-7, Master Sergeant, like my brother and if I had been able to transition to officer training, I would definitely have been able to become a Captain at a minimum and Major at a maximum. I would have been a career woman in the Air Force. I would have traveled the world from base to base with my husband, Davis, and our children by my side simply enjoying life.

What Happens In Vegas...

I only stayed in Philly for a few weeks and then I packed up my bags and headed to Las Vegas, Nevada to live with my older brother Joseph Jackson Abel.

My brother, Jackson, lived by himself in Las Vegas and was still enlisted in the Air Force, stationed at Nellis Air Force Base. My mother had told my brother that I needed a new start, but she never told him specifically why I was no longer serving in the military, opting instead to tell him that they had simply given me a General Discharge under Honorable Conditions due to the death of my father, our brother and our grandmother's declining health. Jackson accepted that explanation and welcomed me into his home.

During the first several months in Las Vegas, I partied often and slept often as well. I tried to drown my sorrows in loud parties, smoking weed, and cigarettes, drinking as much alcohol as I could stand, and hanging around with happy people all the time. I put all negative thoughts about my experiences out of my mind and focused on trying to have fun, fun, and more fun. Partying hard day-in and day-out was very effective and the alcohol and weed helped to keep my fears at bay. I popped pills, drank as much as possible and I even tried sniffing glue and rush tea for the first time, which was the height of my experimentation during this time of my life. I think rush tea was a concoction mixed with marijuana and some other really bad stuff because it made me so high that I felt like I was flying on a cloud. When you drank this tea, you couldn't stand up, so you had to lie down until the feeling passed. In retrospect, I am actually very glad that my brother was not around most of the time to witness my behavior and the bad choices I was making for myself during this time.

I did not know it at the time, but I was definitely self-medicating. I did anything I could think of to numb the pain of all that I had been through. The assaults in the air force, the funerals, and having sex with my stepbrother while suffering through a deep depression that I wasn't even aware of at the time. I was basically trying to be a free spirit. Hoping to just disappear inside myself and come out the other side as a different version of me.

Years later I learned through therapy that my behavior of having sex with multiple partners is not unheard of in victims of sexual assault and rape suffering from post-traumatic stress disorder. Every time I had sex, I came home and cried myself to sleep, yelled at myself in the mirror, wrote angry words about myself in my journal where I called myself a skank, whore, loose woman, trifling, nasty, stupid and many other derogatory terms for letting myself be used again and again and again.

I remember telling my therapist years later, that after my assaults, I chose to have sex because I was in control in those situations. The men were no longer controlling my body. I told the man what to do and what not to do so they were forced to do what I told them to do, not the other way around. In my mind this meant that no one could take anything from me if I was giving it to them, right? WRONG! My actions were just another way of numbing myself from the pain of being raped and assaulted during my time of service.

For the most part, my brother Jackson allowed me to hang out and everything worked out well for about a couple of months because he was often on TDY (Temporary Duty Yonder) for weeks at a time. TDY simply meant that he would be stationed at base locations other than his permanent base (Nellis AFB) for weeks at a time performing his job on a temporary basis.

I COUNT THE DARK

My brother's last TDY ended about several months after I had arrived in Las Vegas my brother noticed how much time I spent partying and sleeping, and he decided it was time for me to get a job. I applied for several jobs and the first job I got was as a telemarketer. It was an easy job, all I had to do was call up different people, read a script and try to make a sale. It was not the best job in the world and the pay wasn't great, but it kept me out of the apartment and kept my brother off my back.

I went to Vegas because I needed to be taken care of and protected. To be around someone I respected and around someone who loved me unconditionally. His value in my life ran neck and neck with my mother and in a way even surpasses that, and he has unique experiences being a soldier in Vietnam and a lifelong air force sergeant, and he could understand some of what I experienced. I had been dictated to by the higher-ups and then booted out, and my military career was over. He had made the military work, he had worked it and made it his career. I felt like a failure, and believed it was all my fault – no one else could possibly be to blame.

Normalcy???

After a while, I started to feel a little better about myself and I began to realize that being a telemarketer was not the job for me I felt that I deserved better. I applied for a few bank teller jobs and was very pleased when I secured a job at Nevada National Bank as a bank teller and then later at First Federal Savings and Loan.

I finally started to feel as if I had some control over my life and a new normal came about where I was able to look forward to waking up every morning and going to work. I no longer felt that sense of dread that I used to feel every morning dragging myself out of bed to face another hopeless day. I started to make more friends and this time they were true friends that knew how to have fun just dancing and hanging out at different people's houses throwing barbecues with only a little bit of drinking thrown in for good measure.

For the next few years, I found the best way to turn my life around was found in surround myself with positive people, a good job, good fun, and family. I took time during every holiday break and vacation to go for long hikes in the mountains, jet-skiing on Lake Mead, enjoying the snow in Reno, Nevada at the ski resorts as well as visiting family in Los Angeles, California, and taking trips back home to Philadelphia, Pennsylvania.

After a while, I focused less on the bad things that had happened to me and focused on living a good life. It was hard in the beginning but the more I worked at, it the easier it became to feel better about my life. I didn't realize until years later that I had buried my trauma so that I could function in the world. Every one of us can bury traumatic experiences, enabling us to function as competent adults in society. It is part of our normal fight or flight response, which is built into each of us. I did not know at the time that all my attempts at partying hard were just an exercise in self-preservation, but I shudder to think of what a mess I would have been, had I not surrounded myself with warm and nurturing people.

During the next few years, I experienced healthy job progression. I left Nevada National Bank and was hired as a bank teller at First Federal Savings and Loan, where I was promoted multiple times. I had a lot of responsibility and I felt good handling this responsibility as a young black girl. I no longer felt like a little girl from North Philly with no prospects other than to be a young, teenage unwed mother. I had proved to myself that I could overcome all the bad experiences that happened in the past and come out the other side a respectable young woman with a blossoming career far from the streets of North Philly.

A Memoir? Be Careful, Tina

A lazy Sunday afternoon, and I'm sitting in the living room back in Philly watching a television show, nothing memorable, just something to fill the void in the day before I start dinner. The house phone rings, getting up from the navy-blue, cloth-colored armchair that sits in the corner, I take two steps to get to the phone that sits on the left-hand shelf of the fake-maple wood and glass entertainment center. I answer on the third ring, "Hello?"

"Tina?"

"It's me, Jackson."

Smiling, I answered with a, "Duh, I know it's you because I know your voice. What's up, big bro?" I asked as I sank to the floor to get more comfortable. The telephone cord doesn't stretch all the way over to the chair so I could either stand up and talk or take a seat on the floor. I chose to sit on the floor. I can hear my brother sigh through the phone as he says, "Nothing." I was just sitting here thinking about Mom, and I remembered something that I forgot to mention. Did I tell you that I had already gotten mom her own apartment for when she was going to come back here?"

Hearing that made me sit up straight, raising my eyebrows, I said, "What? Mama was going to come back there and stay in an apartment?"

"Yep, we applied to a retirement community, and the envelope came the other day saying that her spot was finally available. I breathed in a sigh, a teardrop falling to my cheek as I inhaled saying, "Wow, that's too much Jackson, just too much. If only Mama had lived longer, she would have been out there with you enjoying all that good weather and having lots of no-stress days before she died."

Jackson, "Yea, I know but that didn't happen so….I just wanted to tell someone, so I called to tell you. It kinda took me off guard and hit me hard so I had to tell someone, you know?" Swallowing hard, I said, "Yea, I know. I've been going through some things here myself just thinking back on how everything happened so fast and all of us not really having enough time to process her illness first, and then she's gone before we even know it. Shifting my legs from one side to sit cross-legged on the floor, I say, "Jackson, you know I'm writing a book, don't you?"

Jackson asks, "A book? Nah, I didn't know that Tina. What are you going to write about? Mom?"

"Well, a part of the book will be about Mom but much of the book will be about me and my time in the Air Force."

"Oh, ok."

I shifted and came to a standing position for this next part because I didn't know what Jackson would say when the next words came out of my mouth. Letting out a long exhale, I said, "Yea, I'm writing about my assault in the Air Force. You know that I have a service-connected disability from in the Air Force, don't you?"

"No, I didn't know that. Hmmmm. Ok. Ok." I hurried up to get through this part of the conversation and said, "Yea, I submitted my disability claim to the VA and after a couple of years they approved me. I've been going to therapy over the last few years to help me deal with my PTSD and now I feel strong enough to write about my experiences."

"Ok. Ok. Tina, well just be careful you know. You never know what could happen once you finish writing it and get it out there."

"Yea, I know, I'll be careful. Well, I'mma go now because I've got to fix something for dinner for these kids."

"Yea ok, Tina. Well then, I'll talk to you later. Ok? You take care of yourself, ok?"

"Ok, big bro, I'll be careful and take care of myself. Talk to you soon."

Hanging up the phone, I walked back to the chair, plopping down, I wondered what Jackson really thought about what I said about the Air Force. My brother was a career Air Force and never said a bad word about his time in the Service. He did not ask me any questions when I mentioned being attacked and while that might seem strange to someone else, it was actually what I expected from my brother because he has always been a very matter-of-fact person. He doesn't say a lot and he chooses his words carefully. He doesn't like to dwell on the negative and he's very solution oriented. Now that I think about it, I also don't see him even reading my book because he would see no point in reviewing a hurtful point in my past. He would always rather that I focus on the lighter side of life.

Davis – Back In Love, Again

Things with Davis picked up little by little, and I found myself back in Philly, working and just living life. Everything between us seemed to be working out fine, that is until one day when I got off work and went straight over to Davis's grandmother's house, he met me at the door with a concerned look on his face. Leaning in while taking my bag off my shoulder, I kissed his warm, sweet lips saying, "What's up babe? Why the look of concern? It can't be that bad."

Kissing me back and helping me off with my coat, Davis closed the door and said, "Come on upstairs, there's something I have to tell you."

Noticing Auntie in the kitchen making dinner in her loose beige checkered button-down top and a pair of loose-fitting beige slacks on, I ran in quickly just to grab a hug before heading upstairs. Auntie leaned her head back into me as I kissed her left cheek and gave her a quick squeeze from behind. As I turned to run back to the steps, I heard Auntie yell out, "Dinner will be done in a few minutes so yaw'll come right back down here, hear? Don't be up there messin' around and stuff."

I took the steps quickly, "Okay," I hollered back.

As usual, the stairs creaked as I ran up, so I had to hold onto the rickety banister just to make sure I didn't trip on the stairs. Davis's bedroom was at the back of the house but since the house was so small it only took me about four or five steps once I hit the top landing and I was in his room. The room was cramped with all of his DJ equipment, big black speakers, and albums so there wasn't much room for anything else other than his twin bed, bedside table, and a small lamp.

Davis was putting an album on the turntable when I plopped down on the bed. He cleared his throat and turned toward me.

"So, DJ's mom wants to come back around so I met with her today to talk about DJ."

DJ was Davis's son with XX. I raised my eyebrows and screwed up my face but before I could say a word, Davis interrupted. "Don't worry, she didn't come upstairs. We spoke outside the house."

I exhaled and leaned back against the pillow to let him continue. Davis hung his head just a little and then glanced up at me. "I told her that I don't want her anymore and that you and I are back together but she just got upset, started cussing and as she was cussing, I just turned around and came back inside the house."

I leaned forward, reaching up to pull him down on the bed next to me. "Wow! That must have been deep. What did she think was going to happen?"

Earth, Wind, and Fire was just blowing and "Reasons" was playing all nice and low as the irony of the song was not lost on me. She really thought she still had a chance. Davis was biting his lip and I put my finger to his lips to get him to stop. "I hope she got the message and maybe she won't bother us anymore."

Davis stood quickly turning back to switch up the album/song and put on The Gap Band, "Yearning for Your Love" nice and low. Davis grabbed my hand and pulled me in for a quick kiss, "Yeah, I hope so, but you know she's unpredictable. She was yelling through the door, threatening me, telling me I would be sorry and you and Auntie too, so I told Auntie to make sure she doesn't go out alone without me just to make sure she doesn't try anything."

Motherhood Rule#1-Protect Your Children

A few days passed, and we hadn't heard any more from her, so Davis told Auntie and me that everything was most likely okay. A few days later, I dropped my son off with Auntie in the morning as usual and went to work. Davis had started back up at work, so he wasn't getting home most nights until close to 8:00 pm while most evenings I arrived at Auntie's around 5:45 or 6:00 pm and just waited around for him to get home before I packed up my young man and headed back to Mom's.

One day, I got off the El at 52nd and Market and walked up 52nd to Lindenwold. The sun was still shining bright because it was almost summertime, and it was setting later in the day. Auntie's house was only a few feet from the corner so when I rounded the corner of her block I was across the street in minutes. As I walked up to my car, which was parked directly in front of her door, I glanced at it. Once I was at Auntie's front door, I gasped, as the top half of the door was covered with cardboard: the pane had been broken. I rang the bell and called for Auntie, and she opened the door quickly to pull me inside.

I was always surprised by Auntie's strength because she seemed so frail. She pulled me in for a big hug. "Okay, I'm okay. Now, don't you start getting upset at what I'm about to tell you. Davis is on his way home now. The police just left, and they took her to jail."

I had no idea what she was talking about. "Cops? What happened to the glass in the door?"

Auntie was still holding my shoulders. "Come on, let's sit down."

The couch took up almost all of the small living room and was covered in thick plastic that everyone used to protect their "good furniture" back in the day. Auntie always wore slacks except on Sunday when she went to church so today was no different. She wore a pair of slacks with a light pink, button-down shirt underneath her frilly white apron with red roses all over it. She lifted the top of the apron over her head and let it fall to her waist as we were sitting facing each other on the sofa. Frowning a little, she grabbed both my hands in hers and started talking. "That crazy girl, DJ's mother, came over here today cutting up, talking about how she was going to make Davis sorry for not letting her see DJ last time she was over here. I told her to get on away from my door with her mess – shouted at her through the screen door – and then she yelled, 'Tell Davis he better call me now before I shoot up this place.'"

My hands were starting to get a little numb as Auntie was still holding them in a vice grip while she was talking, so I gently stretched my fingers, and Auntie finally released her grip, apologizing for holding my hands so tightly. I glanced toward the vestibule again. "But what happened to the door? I still don't understand."

Auntie turned to look at the door again, "I walked away from the front door just in time, and as I was walking back to the kitchen, I heard a sound and then another sound followed by the shattered glass falling to the floor. I almost jumped outta my skin. I waited a few minutes before going to the door and walked over to the vestibule door. Before I could reach out for the doorknob the rest of the glass in the door frame just fell to the floor. I guessed that dumb girl musta thrown something through the door and then ran. I called the cops and then I called Davis and told him what happened so he's on his way home now. Next, I called Jaime down here and had him help me clean up all the glass."

Jaime was Davis's older brother and he was always home. Auntie said that once Jaime had put up some cardboard and newspaper on the vestibule and front door that she opened the door to the police and that's when they told her what happened to my car. I started to get up but before I could stand, I felt Auntie pulling me back down again telling me to calm down. After a few moments, I heard the front door open and Davis came rushing in, and the look on his face told me how angry he was about what had happened. He rushed over and hugged us both, and then yelled for Jaime to come downstairs. Davis took my hand and walked me to the front door. "Jaime and I are going to clean up the car, okay, and you'll be able to drive it no problem because I started it up when I got here even before coming in the house."

We went out to stand on the porch, and I was just shaking as I looked at the passenger side of my car. The rear window was splintered and I could see a hole in the middle of the fractured glass. Davis was holding onto me and without speaking he unlocked the car and walked me down the steps to open the rear door on the passenger side. I didn't realize it, but tears were running down my cheeks and then I leaned in and noticed that there was a hole in the very top of my son's car seat and I almost lost it right there.

"Davis, what did she do to my car?"

His ex-girlfriend, the mother of his son Dj, had shot up my car windows and destroyed Auntie's front door. The gunshot went directly through the driver's side door of my car, on an angle, slicing through my son's car seat and exiting through the rear window. That was enough of a sign to convince me that Davis and I were not meant to be together at this point in my life, so after a while, we broke things off again and both went our separate ways. Basically, I found it difficult to continue going over there to see him, given that there had been a potential threat to my son's life.

As much as I loved Davis, I had a clear responsibility to protect my son. As it was, Davis and I were not really on solid footing anymore after having had so many disruptions in our lives during those years; any little thing was likely to come along and break us apart. Neither one of us could have anticipated that Dj's mother would be the cause of our last breakup.

That engagement ring colored the remainder of our relationship. I felt like a failure even though I did not really do anything wrong in this instance. I was to blame because I had the lost the ring, and even though I knew he loved me deeply and wanted a life with me, somehow, we just couldn't get past that lost ring.

It was during this point in my life that I met the man who would soon be my husband, Sean Patrick. In my romantic relationships with Sean and, much later on, Ellis, there was always something missing, something that was indefinable and indescribable. I tried to figure out what was wrong in my life, but I could not come up with a reasonable explanation, so I just carried on moving in whatever direction life seemed to take me up until the death of my mother, Ruth, at the age of 69.

The Unraveling...

When my mother died on June 26, 2001, I began to feel my armor crack and that was the beginning of my walls starting to crumble. For many years, my mother held me together as I moved from job to job; from apartment to apartment; from state to state, and from one relationship to another. Ruth was always there to help me pick up the pieces when things went wrong. She was the one strong shoulder on which I could always lean. My mother was there for every important moment in my life up until her death.

My mother was there for me when I cooked my first Thanksgiving Day turkey for my brother Jackson, his girlfriend, and myself in November 1981. I was so young and dumb back then because I thought that all I had to do was put the turkey in the oven and that it would cook itself without me having to worry about it. I remember putting the turkey in the oven, leaving to go attend a bridal shower, and coming back home to fire trucks and firemen coming out of my apartment because a neighbor had reported a fire in my apartment. The firemen determined that it was only smoke coming from the spilled turkey juice in the oven, so all was not lost. I received a stern talking too from the firemen and the apartment manager and learned a very important lesson – buy a bigger pan for the turkey, so the juice doesn't spill out all over the inside of the oven. Now the lesson I should have learned was 'don't go out to a bridal shower when you are cooking a Thanksgiving Day Dinner too funny.

I had a great job at the time at the Federal Reserve Bank of Philadelphia; I was earning a very good salary, one that enabled me to be able to take care of my four children nicely as a recently divorced woman. Marriage to Sean was easy at first and full of fun, as all marriages should be in the beginning; however, as we settled into our married life and I gave birth to our two children, a beautiful girl and then a handsome little boy, life began to turn problematic. We experienced some of the normal growing pains that all marriages experience when money is tight, and the needs of the family outweigh the needs of the individual partners, so my husband turned to other women and his video games for solace. In turn, I found comfort in our children and discovered that in this role I excelled as it gave me more joy than I was receiving in my marriage.

Now I realize that in my relationship with Davis and with my husband as well, I subconsciously sabotaged those relationships. I allowed the stigma of being raped and sexually assaulted to color all my future relationships. I know for a fact that I have great difficulty trusting men in any relationship whether it was professional or personal and this lack of trust crossed boundaries into other aspects of my life, so the assaults in the military adversely affected my experiences. Lack of trust and traumatic events in life can, in fact, alter how we behave in relationships with other people.

My trauma affected my ability to rebound in my relationship with Davis. The gunshot through my car window presented me with a perfect opportunity to run away from the relationship even though the shooter was arrested and imprisoned for her actions and was no longer a threat to myself or my child. My trauma also affected my marriage: the unconditional love of my children was a stronger refuge for me than was the love of my husband.

One of Sean's girlfriends began to harass me via phone calls, and that caused us to argue more and more. After a while, I just couldn't take it anymore and I asked Sean to move out and told him that I was filing for a divorce.

I chose to divorce my husband after a few years because of his extra-marital affairs and his constant mental abuse. He took every chance to blame me for his affairs by telling me that I let myself go after having our children and that I spent more time with the kids than I spent with him. While he was right about how much time I spent with the kids, I felt that since I had a nine-year-old and two children under three that I should be spending as much time as possible with them.

Before I filed, I talked to my mother and after lots of long conversations, she agreed with me that divorce might be my only option. She did not like hearing of Sean's affairs and how he was spending less and less time at home helping me out with the kids. I even tried to talk things over with Sean's mom as well, but no matter the well-meaning advice received, I found that I could not forgive him for everything that had happened. I was much to hurt at the time to follow anyone's sage wisdom so here was yet another failed relationship and I was barely 35 years old.

After my divorce, I was alone for several years and I spent most of those years just focusing on raising my children and keeping a decent job. The next relationship I had was with Ellis F. Harmon and he became the father of my fourth child, a nine-pound beautiful baby girl. I find it very interesting that Ellis was a psychotherapist and that he seemed to enjoy trying to diagnose my woes. No matter what he did, though, he never succeeded in helping me through my trust issues and shortly after the birth of our daughter, he and I ceased to be a couple any longer. He did the best he could to remain a part of his daughter's life, though.

At this point in my life, I was feeling no pain, as they say, and I was optimistic that my life would only get better, and then my mother died. Once my mother died just a little over nine months after my fourth child was born, everything in my world began to look just a little bit bleak.

RuthieMae Ford-Green-Reed, lifted up

My mother died of breast and lung cancer. When she was first stricken with cancer, the only one she told was my big brother, Jackson. She left Philadelphia in the early spring of 2001, February; I believe to go see my big brother Jackson in Las Vegas and did not return until Memorial Day 2001. When my mother came back home, she had to be rushed to the hospital the very next day because her blood pressure was very high.

It turned out that her pressure was high because she was experiencing spasms of pain brought on by cancer racking through her body. I, along with my other siblings did not know that she was sick because she kept it from all of us except Jackson so when the doctor's diagnosis came back telling me that it was Stage 4 Cancer, I was shocked. The doctors told me that my mother had less than one month to live. The decision was made for mama to stay in the hospital so that the doctors could keep her as comfortable as possible. The only other recourse would have been for her to come home with me, and I would have done my best to try to manage palliative care at home.

Mama's care would have been left up to me mostly because most of my siblings were living out of the city at this point (Jackson, Rita, and Shelly) or involved in drugs (like my brother Little Junior and Jason) and simply unable to help. At this point in my life, I was divorced and living alone raising four children, so it would have been hard to handle everything on my own, but I would have gladly done it without regrets but after speaking with my brother Jackson, he and I decided it was best for her to be in the hospital.

As the shock of my mother's illness continued to ripple through me, I also instinctively went into fight-or-flight mode again and began trying to figure out how to make my mother's last days on this earth palatable, comfortable, and with the least amount of added stress as possible. Having to help her handle all her business affairs gave me something to do and helped to put off my own stress at realizing that my mother was no longer going to be with me.

The days went by slowly at first which I was most grateful for because I needed as much time as possible to figure out how to tell my children and gather all my other siblings around so that we could all figure everything out. After everyone came together, we spoke about everything and everyone agreed that I should handle her affairs since Mama was living with me anyway and my other siblings thought that should make it easier to get things done.

I spent every evening with Mama and most mornings I would stop by before I went to work. My job position at the Federal Reserve was classified as 'exempt' which meant that I didn't have to punch the clock like non-exempt workers. My hours were flexible, so I was ok so long as I worked 7.5 hours a day, therefore, I was able to work my schedule around my mother's illness. After the initial shock wore off the days seemed to pick up speed and the days were filled with people stopping by the hospital to see Mom; she received a gazillion phone calls from everyone wishing her well and hoping for a miracle and a speedy recovery.

The days finally started coming to an end and the closer the days became the stronger I began to feel. I felt that I had to be strong for my mother because she was starting to be a little fearful about leaving me alone. We had many long talks and made many lists telling me what to do when this happened and what to do if that happened. I was as prepared as I could possibly be all the way up to the very end. I was with my mother until she took her last breath and I heard the rattle in her chest that people often speak of as the 'death rattle'. I pronounced my mother dead at 2:57 pm on June 26, 2001; however, the doctors pronounced her dead at 3:05 pm because that's when they entered the room and examined her to proclaim her death. They can say 3:05 all they want but I know when my mother died because I was the only one in the room.

Once my mother was pronounced, I had to wait a while until they came to take her body away, and while I was waiting, my church mothers just happened to come into the room for a visit. Their arrival, almost right on queue was perfect as it was almost as if they knew it was time to lift Momma up in prayer and send her on her heavenly journey.

In walked Mom-Mom Catherine Foreman, Mom Mavis Robinson, and my beloved Momma Alma Woodard. These ladies, along with my First Lady, Dr. Juliet Campbell-Farrell are the titans of intercessory prayer in my book. When you are prayed over and by Mom-Mom Foreman, Mom Robinson, Momma Woodard and First Lady, Dr. Juliet Campbell-Farrell, you know your prayers will be answered in due time simply because of their intercession. It was Momma Woodard who first brought me into the bosom of my church family at Wynnefield Presbyterian Church, with Reverend Paul Farrell, presiding pastor, then and now. At the time, Momma Woodard was giving me counsel as she helped me learn how to handle the difficulties encountered during the separation from my then-husband, Sean Johnson.

As they set out to surround me and mama, lying still in her bed, they each took the time, one by one, to draw me into an intense hug and squeeze my hand before settling into position. In those moments, I could feel the spirits starting to dance in the room as the angels began gathering in anticipation of Momma's arrival into heaven. I can tell you that if you have never experienced a 'praying mother or praying grandmother' you don't know what you are missing because Mama Catherine, Mama Mavis, and Mama Alma were all the praying Mamas I needed that day.

They prayed and prayed and prayed all my sad tears away. I felt a smile begin to spread across my face as I felt mama's spirit begin to lift upward, flying softly up through the ceiling, up through the floors of concrete, steel, and metal until she was soaring through the clouds to be with our god.

Once all the praying had subsided, I was able to finally let them take mama's body out of the room because I knew then that she was no longer occupying that body and that her soul had been lifted up. At that moment, I knew intently what Philippians 4:7 *peace that surpasses all understanding* truly meant because although momma was gone, I felt no pain, I was supremely calm and smiled freely as I hugged all my praying mommas.

Yes, momma had made her transition, and it was extremely difficult during the process, yet because I was able to be there with her and help allay her fears, I believe she was able to reconcile herself with God's will when she took her last breath.

I take immense pride in being able to help her transition as she said her goodbyes to everyone that she loved that she knew she was leaving behind. During her final moments she was not able to speak audibly but we had our own language and when the last loved one's name was spoken, she looked up at me expectantly, eyes fluttering wildly as if to say, 'Wait, what about you? Berthienna? I have not said goodbye to you my sweet girl. I knew even without her questioning glances that she wanted to make sure that I would be ok without her strong arms around me to hold me up on my remaining journey of life. I kissed her forehead, her fluttering, tear-soaked eyes and hugged her ever so gently as I told her, "I love you, Mama-dear so very, very much and yes, I will be just fine."

A thin smile spread across her lips, a few more tears escaped her fluttering eyelids and in the smallest of breaths she was gone on to glory. Helping my mother ease into her transition is one of the greatest and most special moments of our life together. Just as she was the giver of life to me and the first to witness me take a breath, I felt so blessed to have been there with her sharing her last breath on this earth. I will forever cherish those moments never forgetting our special time together there at the end. As I watched her ease into her transition, I felt more grounded than I had felt in my life before or sense that fateful day.

I left the hospital feeling better than when I had arrived that morning because I had an assurance that I had never felt before as I now knew that I could handle the funeral arrangements just fine.

In the moments just following the prayer, I felt as if I could handle anything that life was about to throw at me. Somehow, I had overcome my past fears of inadequacy, the shame of being victimized at an early age while serving in the military, my failing marriage, everything somehow was no longer an issue for me and that left me with a feeling of being cleansed. Being prayed over by my church mothers was one of the most powerful and profound moments of my life and a moment that I will always treasure. This is my living testimony – having faith and believing in the miracle of prayer is definitely my recommendation for curing whatever ails you.

My brother Jackson and I handled all the financial affairs concerning the funeral and I handled the church ceremony. I picked out Mama's dress, shoes, pantyhose and even applied her makeup the right way because the funeral home mortician didn't know how to apply the eyebrow pencil to Mama's eyebrows the right way. You see Mama didn't have any eyebrows because she chose to pluck them most of her life and pencil them on with a black eyebrow pencil. Upon meeting my mother, everyone would always comment on her beautiful eyes, her high cheekbones, her marvelously smooth skin, and her beautiful scent.

Whenever you hugged my mother, you always came away with the sweet, soft scent of Jergens lotion mixed with whatever fragrance she was enamored with at the time. In the early days, it was usually Jean Nate, followed by Chanel No 5, Emeraude by Coty, Fracas by Jake Piguet, and lastly, Allure by Chanel in her final days. No matter what perfume my mother wore, the fragrance became her and her soft scent lingered on after she left the room.

Mama's homegoing service was absolutely wonderful and the church was full, every seat in every pew taken up by family, friends, and well-wishers. I was so happy to see everyone in attendance giving Mama a great send-off.

After the funeral, life seemed to settle down again and I was in full motherhood swing, so I didn't have time to feel too sad, angry, or depressed at the cards that life seemed to have dealt me. I carried on at work and continued to take care of the kids without too many hiccups.

In 2002, I was laid off from my job and things started to get hard to handle at home. I can just about see the crack in my armor starting to wind its way down further and further along my spine. As the years swam by, I managed to keep my head up, but my armor was cracking just a little bit more as life handed me the usual twists and turns out, I managed to not fall into severe depression, but it was getting harder and harder to maintain a smile on my face. **In 2012, that tiny little crack that had started growing when Mama died—it exploded.**

Matthews ... My VA Guide

In the summer of 2012, I was sitting at home at the dining room table just fiddling around with my computer when I stumbled upon an article discussing an incident involving Sexual Assault that had occurred in the military. I don't remember the title of the article as much as I remember what the article was stating about sexual assault occurring at a military installation in the present day. I can recall starting to shake and the feel of the warm tears rolling down my face and then becoming so mad instantly that I closed the lid on my computer and just bowed my head at the table.

A few moments later I was startled by the ringing of my cell phone and so I gathered myself together as much as I could and answered the phone. Matthews was on the phone asking me if I could come over and have a drink with him. I knew right away that a drink was not all he wanted if he really cared about the drink at all, so I smiled the fake smile I usually give (in person) through the phone and said, "Sure, coming right over."

At the moment, I didn't care that he just wanted to have sex because I wanted something to take my mind off of the article I just read, and Matthews would do the trick, so I went knowing full well where the night was headed. As usual, the trip to his house was thankfully uneventful and as soon as I parked my car in North Philly, I called him on my phone to let him know that I was outside. Matthews did not seem to have a doorbell that I could ring, and I always felt self-conscious as I stood on the top step of the stoop waiting for him to let me in. I, somehow, always felt as if everyone outside on his block was staring at me saying to themselves... "Humph! There goes another one going in that man's house and you know they just going in there to have sex!"

I always felt dirty going over to see him, and I had never really stopped to think of why I would feel that way when there were many times that we did not have sex but instead, we just watched old black-and-white cowboy shows on his tv, had lots and lots of vodka and orange juice (or whatever juice he happened to have around in the fridge) and just talked about the work or anything that was happening in the world at the time.

Ok, it did not take him long this time to open the door and let me inside. As soon as he closed the door behind me. I had to stop suddenly just to adjust my eyes from the brightness outside (it was almost 7 pm on a sunny summer's evening, so there was still a lot of sunshine outside) to the interior darkness that swallowed me up in the little entryway just before stepping up to his interior door which was only partially cracked open.

Matthews quickly stepped up beside me, reached over my shoulder, and pushed the door open further so that I could see to step inside. Once inside, I am greeted by his chocolate brown loveseat to the left of me, and I glance at it and notice its full to the brim with clothes tossed all over it, a pillow with a light blue pillow cover on it, some loose weights that I assume he had been working out with just before he called me, maybe and his laptop was perched on top of everything, a bit too precariously if you ask me, but it wasn't my laptop so what did I care if it was knocked over.

As I was stepping to my right to get closer to the sofa and sit down, I felt Matthews reach around from behind me and cup my two breasts in his hands, pulling me back towards him. I could tell from that move that he was already a bit drunk and ready to hit the bed, but I pulled away from him just as quickly and said, "Hold on, my brother, where's my drink? I want to get tipsy, too, since it seems like you started without me."

I was grinning as I said it, and I saw a smile light up his face as he stepped back to give me space and then just as quickly said, "Coming right up, my lady," walking into his dining room to pour me a drink.

I watched as he poured a healthy dose of vodka into a red plastic cup (most likely a 20 oz cup because Matthews never did anything halfway like a normal person would and kept a supply of 8oz or maybe even 12 oz cups. Matthews's cups were always 20 oz. or larger.) I chuckled silently, just shaking my head from left to right several times, and moved to hand the cup to me when I had to stop him again, saying, "Whoa. Where's my ice? My juice? You know I can't drink that stuff straight like you. Come on now, Matthews."

He just smiled, laughed a little, and said, "Oh, I knew I forgot something- Be right back."

I watched him take about three steps, walk towards the fridge in his small kitchen with my cup in hand, and set my cup down on top of the fridge as he reached into the freezer for the ice cube tray. I stopped him right there and asked him to just bring the tray to me so I could add my own ice cubes since I already knew he was only going to put a few cubes in the cup, which would not have been enough ice for me. Matthews just smiled, grabbed my cup and the tray, and walked back to the dining room table to set it down. I saw him reach for his cup, and before he could put it to his lips, I stopped him again, saying, "Juice?"

Matthews motioned to the fridge as he put his lips to his cup, took a big gulp, and then he returned to the sofa in the living room and sat down while I finished preparing my drink. I grabbed the only juice I saw in the fridge (the last bit of a half-gallon jug of Apple Juice), added about six ice cubes to my cup, and then filled the rest up with apple juice. Whoever heard of drinking vodka with apple juice as a chaser/mixer? I never had that was for sure, but it was better than a blank. I drank almost half of the drink right away – tasting a ton of vodka all the way but I had to do that because

I desperately needed to add the last bit of apple juice in the cup to try to tone down the drink as best I could. It didn't help much, but it helped a little, making the drink just a little bit more palatable.

My Hard Truth

I joined Matthews on the sofa watching an episode of one of his favorites –'Bonanza' starring Lorne Greene, Pernell Jakes, and Michael Landon. Those 'Cartwrights' were always known for holding it down, keeping us all glued to the television sets back in the day. We both sat there for a few moments quietly, just sipping and sipping on our drinks. Then suddenly, Matthews turns to me and says, "Ok, that's enough of that, come on."

He stood up, and so did I, and then we walked thru the dining room, then the kitchen, then a second room (which I never ever asked him what the room was used for because most of the time there were just odds and ends in the room, pretty much like this time) and finally we were in the bedroom. The lights were off in all of the rooms we walked thru, in addition to his bedroom, so I had to hold his hand as we were walking just to follow him and not trip on anything. Entering the bedroom, there was just enough light coming from the television that I could make out the outline of the bed, covers were already pulled back as we stepped into the room. We both split, with Matthews walking to my left and me walking to the right side of his bed, placing my drink on the floor, and we began stripping off our clothes.

It had always been just like that sip a few sips of a drink, watch a little bit of tv and then walk back to his bedroom, undress, and screw. There were times in-between when we might share a few quick kisses in the living room, grope each other a bit, and then head to the bedroom, but most of the time it was sip, tv, undress, and screw. But for some reason, that night, it just felt different the moment I got back to his bedroom. I had taken off my top and pants and stopped then to finish off my drink before taking any other clothes off.

I turned and asked Matthews if he had a Heineken (he knew to always keep Heineken handy for me because I liked to have a bottle or two before, during, and after sex). I especially liked to fill my mouth with a cold beer and take him just to feel the dichotomy between the warmth and the cold. Matthews had already slipped under the covers but threw off the covers just as quickly, standing and walking away from me, saying, "Coming right up, babe."

I stared at his naked behind as he walked out of the room and came back in a flash with a very cold open bottle of Heineken in his hand. The bottle was so cold when he gave it to me that my fingers were almost instantly stuck to the bottle. You know the way that happens because your hand is much warmer than the coldness of the bottle and when there is the slightest bit of frost in the bottle, it will make your fingers sort of freeze and get stuck to the side of the bottle. I always found that funny, but that night even that didn't make me smile or laugh. As a matter of fact, it actually startled me when I reached up grabbed the bottle and took it from him.

Sitting up in his bed, taking sips of the Heineken, Matthews started flipping the channels on his tv, found some movie to play, started it, and turned to take the bottle out of my hands. I let him take the bottle out of my hands, and then we started kissing and fondling each other. The more aroused I noticed Matthews became, the less aroused I was. After a few minutes, he noticed something was wrong, stopped touching me, reached down for my bottle of Heineken, and gave it to me, asking me what was wrong all in one motion.

Out of nowhere, these tears welled up in my eyes and I started to cry. I could tell that my crying made him uncomfortable, but he sat there silently and let me cry it out. After a while, he got up, walked a few steps into his bathroom and I could hear water running (the bathroom was the very last room and each room was connected to one another, so he only had to take a couple of steps to get inside the bathroom). He returned in a few seconds and offered me a warm washcloth to wipe my face. I took it, and it felt so good on my face that it helped calm me down the rest of the way since I had pretty much already finished crying it all out.

I felt a little embarrassed but not too bad because Matthews was…well…Matthews, so it's okay for him to see me break down. I could always be real with him. Before I knew it, I started laughing and apologizing to him at the same time for coming over and crying all over him. He turned to look at me, "No problem, sweetie. Now, what happened? What had you all upset? I know it wasn't anything I said, so it had to be something else." He turned back to the movie and took a sip of his drink.

"Do you mind if we go back to the living room? I asked.

He replied, "No problem."

As I started putting my clothes back on, I glanced at Matthews and noticed he had put his pants back on and was already walking back toward the living room, so I quickly gathered up my sneakers and followed him back into the other room with my beer in my other hand. I paused in the kitchen to open the fridge, reach up into the freezer, and grabbed another Heineken. I stopped in the dining room, put my sneakers on the floor, and stepped into each one while I glanced around for the bottle opener that Matthews must have used. He noticed me looking around and said, "Oh, it's back in the bedroom on the floor beside the bed."

I said, "Ok," turned and walked back to the bedroom to retrieve the bottle opener.

Once I returned, I opened the Heineken, immediately took a swig, and started telling Matthews about the article I was reading just before he called me to come over. He was looking at me the whole time I was speaking, and when I finished, he said, "Ok. So, help me understand why that article messed up my night, and I couldn't get my groove on," he said with almost a half chuckle/smile on his face.

I realized then that I had never told him about being attacked in the military, so of course, he couldn't understand. I said, "Don't you think that's horrible what happened to those women in the military?"

He answered, "Yes, I agree, it was/is horrible, but I still don't see what that has to do with right now."

I could tell that he was softening and being more sympathetic, but I couldn't figure out how to get the words out of my mouth, so I mumbled something about needing to get home, thanked him for the drinks, and walked towards the door to leave. Matthews stood up and grabbed my hand as I walked past him and turned me around to face him. He looked me square in the eye and said, "Raincheck?"

I said, "Sure, raincheck. Talk to you later," giving him a peck on the cheek.

I left quickly, walked to my car, got in, and drove away. All the way home I was beating myself up with feelings of shame, anger, confusion, and then befuddlement. Why didn't I tell Matthews what was going on? What would he do? What would be his reaction? Did I think at the time that he wouldn't believe me or that he would think I was dumb for being used? A ton of thoughts were rolling around in my head that kept me company on the ride home. By the time I had parked my car and got in the house, my phone was ringing, and it was Matthews on the phone. He asked me if I was safe in the house and said he wanted to know what was going on. He said he was going to just let it go but couldn't because he thought we both had the same thoughts about what was going to happen that night, so he was basically confused. I told him to give me a few moments and that I would call him back in a few.

I went to the fridge, grabbed a bottle of Pinot Grigio that was halfway gone, poured myself a glass, and then sat down to gather my thoughts. After finishing off that glass and then half of a second glass, I was sufficiently tipsy enough to return Matthews's call. I opened the call with, "Ok, you don't get to say anything until I finish. You just must sit and listen."

Matthews said, "Ok. No problem. I can do that."

I started talking, and before I knew it, Matthews interrupted me saying, "Ok, dearie, let me stop you right there. You don't need to say anything more. I don't need to hear anything else. Now, listen to me. Were you attacked in the military?"

I said, "Yes, I was attacked."

Matthews said, "What you need to do is file a claim with the VA. You can go online and file a claim, and you don't need to see anyone face-to-face or take time off of work to do this because you can just do it from home."

I asked him what he meant by filing a claim. What would filing a claim do for me?

He said, "Did you ever file a claim with the VA before? Did you ever tell anyone what happened?"

I said, "I told them back then, but I haven't done anything since I got out of the military. If I had not read that article earlier tonight, I don't think it would have mattered to me because I just don't think about that stuff." '

Matthews said, "Just file a claim. Go to the VA's website, and all the information is there to walk you through filing a claim."

I said, "Ok. I will."

Matthews then asked me if I was ok, again and I said, "Yes, I'm ok."

The next thing out of his mouth caused me to throw my head back abruptly and laugh out loud. In true Matthew's fashion and with no shame in his game, he said, "Good, now get your behind back over here so that I can make love to you real good!"

You could never say that Matthews wasn't a man forever out to get his no matter the time or the place! That he was. That he was. I finished laughing and said, "Aww, sweetie, I wish I could but I'm entirely too drunk to drive. After finishing off those two beers, that strong-ass vodka drink you poured, and then coming home and finishing off two glasses of wine! There is just no way that I can make it over there again tonight, but I promise to come by another time and hook you up. Promise."

I could hear his smile through the phone, tinged with disappointment, but he said, "Ok, babe, I'll check with you later."

"Good night," I said.

"Good night, sweetie. Sleep well."

Oh well, after that conversation, there was nothing left to do but go on upstairs to bed, so that's exactly what I did, leaving thoughts of filing a claim with the VA for another day.

The VA Claims Process... The Beginning

Days and months passed by like they usually did, filled with work, afterschool and weekend activities for the kids, church, a little bit of the Go On Girl Book Club meetings with Ramona, Debra, Simone, Mabel, Rose, Cynthia, and the rest of the gang and life just marched on. I continued to see Matthews off and on, and from time to time, he would ask me if I had filed my claim. I would always respond with, "Soon, I will do it soon. Promise."
He would start to say something else and then thinking better of it would just change the conversation to something else.

Finally, one Saturday afternoon, a few months after Matthews first mentioned filing a claim, I found myself with a few quiet moments to myself and I thought…hmmm, why not sit down and file that claim now. I set up the laptop, opened a bottle of Snapple Apple that I had put in the fridge a few days ago, sat down and put in the website address in the Google search engine from my Firefox web page, and waited for the page to open up. In a flash, the page opened, and I sat staring at it for a few seconds, just trying to figure out how to find the right link for submitting a claim. It only took me a moment or two, but I finally found it and opened the page to where I was supposed to be, and began reading about how to file a claim.

The process seemed easy enough –just type all my information in, review it, and then hit submit for it to be processed. I sat there for a few moments trying to figure out how to begin and when I was ready, I started to type. I had not finished typing more than five or six words when I suddenly realized that my vision was blurry, my hands were shaking, and as I sat staring at the screen, I realized that I couldn't make out any of the words because my eyes were so full of tears.

I started to hyperventilate and just fell over on the keyboard weeping. After a few moments, I lifted my head, closed the lid on the laptop, and started trying to pull myself together. Finally, the crying stopped, and I grabbed a paper towel, blew my nose, and dried my tears. That was the end of that! No more typing for me or trying to file a claim. I couldn't even type up a complete sentence before doubling over with sobs and heavy breathing. I just couldn't do it right then. I vowed silently to myself that I would try again another day to do this and maybe it would be easier.

Over the course of the next four Saturdays, I tried, again and again, to sit down at the laptop to submit my claim. Every Saturday, it was the same cycle repeatedly, but each time I succeeded in typing just a few more words each time until I was able to complete a full paragraph.

These writing attempts continued for the next six months until October 2012, when I was finally able to write down my complete experience in one sitting and upload it to the VA website. The memories were so painful to recall that it took multiple attempts to write them all down in a cohesive manner. After I poured everything out, the façade which I had kept up for over 30 years finally started to crack open, revealing the blistering scabs of hurt, pain, confusion, shame, anger, terror, and sadness. I also began to do some research about women being victimized in the military and came across a disturbing statistic.

According to the African American Policy Forum (AAPF.org) "43 percent of African-American veterans suffer from PTSD, and one in three women in the armed forces is sexually assaulted at some point during her service, nearly twice the rate of the civilian population. Black women generally hold lower ranks than their white male or female counterparts despite having more years of service in some instances. This power imbalance causes Black women to experience sexual harassment and assault at a disproportionate rate." Additionally, "In rape victims, PTSD appears to be a risk factor for revictimization, meaning that those who developed PTSD after being raped are significantly more likely to be raped again, compared to victims who do not develop PTSD (Messman-Moore, Ward, & Brown, 2009)

Those statistics were numbing and I was overwhelmed by how profoundly true they were in my situation, given that I had been victimized repeatedly as an AIC in the USAF and then again later in life. It also was not lost on me that I never had the chance to advance in rank while serving in the Air Force. Because of my assault and the fear of retribution, I was forced out of the military.

My Struggle

After the application was filed, I continued working and raising my children. But I soon began experiencing nightmares. I had difficulty sleeping so I went to my primary doctor to request sleep medication and anti-anxiety medication, as I was having difficulty concentrating at work. He prescribed medication and also suggested that I might be suffering from depression, so he wrote me a referral to a psychiatrist and a psychotherapist. I saw what would become the first of many therapists shortly after I turned 40.

Over the last 22 years, I have been diagnosed as suffering from anxiety, depression, post-traumatic stress disorder (PTSD), high blood pressure, diabetes, obesity, mood disorder, and cyclothymia. I searched out a variety of healing modalities as well, including yoga, mindfulness, arithmomania, EMDR (Eye Movement Desensitization and Reprocessing Therapy), and many other forms of therapy as an in-patient and an out-patient. I learned various breathing techniques and discovered how to recognize my "triggers," the various movements, words, gestures, and situations that would cause me to react often instantly and without discernment.

These triggers might make me hyperventilate, cry at a moment's notice go on spending sprees, or make reckless choices with men. Through these therapeutic avenues, I learned to be kind to myself, to stop judging myself so harshly, and to begin understanding that I was/am a valued member of society, someone worthy of love and respect. Over this time, I suffered through two different hospitalizations to treat my depression and my second suicide attempt. One hospitalization was as a result of being 302'd, which refers to "Section 302" that allows for involuntary mental health assessment and subsequent hospitalization if one is deemed to be a danger to oneself or others. The second hospitalization was voluntary and just as necessary as the first in helping me deal with the trauma caused by my victimization.

My first hospitalization took me utterly by surprise. I had fallen at work and broken my hand, and my manager at work took me to the ER. I was asked a simple question during the intake. "Do you feel safe?" Just hearing that word— "safe"—I fell apart and broke down. I said, "No, I don't feel safe." I felt unsafe in the world; I flashed back to the stairwell, dragged up steps, and jammed into the locker. The fall triggered me into the most moments of being completely vulnerable and unsafe. And so, I was remanded to the Psych Unit. It's still a blur to me: I remember how nice the woman was when she spoke to me, I remember the ambulance and being in Intake in the Psychiatric Unit. I remember that when my clothes came back, there were things missing. I was held for 72 hours, and I don't remember those three days; that span of time is still blocked out for me.

They released me after those 72 hours and I went home to my children and we did not discuss my hospitalization at all. I returned to my counseling sessions at the VA with my psychiatrist, where we began discussing additional treatment options for my mental health. My psychiatrist found an inpatient program at another VA hospital in Maryland, that would allow me to stay for months, but my insurance was denied. And when I learned that I felt I didn't want to live. I made the decision to end the pain so I swallowed pills and alcohol and sat down to wait it out. But then my eldest son came home and I knew I could not leave my children at that moment.

Although I was intent on succumbing to my failures, I donned my 'motherly' hat once again and let him take me to the hospital for my first 'voluntary' placement. I felt like such a failure yet again; I had failed to convince others that I needed this help to be mentally whole. It was a downward spiral into failure. My whole life just felt like a series of failures. I felt that I would never be whole, or cleansed, that I would always be a victim. At that time, I had lost my mother and I felt so alone, yet I was the mother of four children who was supposed to be responsible, raise them, protect them from harm and love on them to the best of my ability.

And yet though I had endured many hardships passing through my twenties, thirties, forties, and into my fifties just to reach a point of being able to function like a normal human being in adult society, I was also afforded the grace to begin my healing journey. I believe my most earnest attempts at recovery came with the help of psychiatrists, nurses, and therapists at the VA Medical Center. It is certainly ironic that the institution responsible for my pain and suffering would one day wind up being the institution that ushered me onto a path of healing, self-reflection, and growth.

Matthews...Returning To The Claims Process

Almost immediately after hitting "Send" on my application submission, I felt like celebrating so naturally, I called my guide – Matthews. Now wouldn't you just know it, the call went straight to voice mail. Not to be thwarted by an unanswered telephone call, I figured I would text him as a follow-up because I was in the mood for a sexual encounter. It only took about a minute, and he texted me back and said, "Come on over RubyRed."

I started grinning, ran upstairs, freshened up, splashed on some perfume, and ran out the door as fast as I could to get over to his house. Finally, I turned the corner onto his block and saw an open spot directly in front of his door, exactly what I needed to see at that moment in time. I didn't even have to text or call him from my phone because as I finished parking, I looked to the left out of my car door window and saw him just standing there in the doorway waiting for me.

He was just as ready to see me as I was to see him. Grinning as I opened the car door, closed it, and walked the few feet up to his steps and inside the door. As the door closed on us Matthews pulled me inside his inner door and started pulling up my shirt as I leaned into him trying to push my body even closer to him as he fondled me all over. We stood there in the middle of his living room tugging on each other and kicking off sneakers, pulling off pants and shirts for what seemed like minutes, but I know was only a few seconds and before you knew it, we were walking, half-running back to his bedroom. I had one sneaker and sock on and one sneaker and sock off, no top, no bra, and Matthews only had on his pants having thrown off his shirt and socks back in the living room. There was no need for alcohol at the moment just the need to get up under his sheets and start exploring each other's bodies with our hands, tongues, everything.

Time passed quickly and then slowly and Matthews and I enjoyed each other, then he made us both a drink, we talked some more. Soon after we were both aroused yet again and made love much slower this time. When we finally came up for air, we realized that it was almost 11 o'clock at night and that we both had to be at work in the morning. I got up out of his bed, went into the bathroom, and washed up so that I could put my clothes back on and get home.

When I came out of the bathroom, Matthews was standing there handing me my underwear. He slowly turned me around motioning for me to hand him my bra and then raising my arms, he helped me into my bra fastening it in the back with care. I made a motion to continue getting dressed but just as quickly as I was stepping into my clothes, Matthews was once again taking then off. As you might imagine, somehow, we wound back up in bed again just so I could let Matthews have one more taste before I left to go home. What a nice way to end a Sunday afternoon that started out normal, then became sad, woeful, and emotionally draining and yet, finally ended up being both physically and emotionally satisfying.

He was helping me with the claim and what I gave him in return was sex; this was a kind of transaction. He was my conduit to the claim, and without his guidance, I don't know that I would have ever gotten it approved. My connection to him was like a lifeline. I needed him to help me submit the claim. It was purposeful and all to that end. I thought I was in control but in retrospect, I see now that I still was not. I felt that I was in command of my life, but in reality, even if I thought I was in control, my actions belie that. I am a survivor of sexual assault, and I know now—though back then I hadn't yet come into this awareness—that much of the time I was having sexual experiences with Matthews, I wasn't in my body. I wasn't present (and using alcohol is part of that).

Matthews was having sex with my body, but in my head, I was in the bed at Dyess in Abilene. I was in that stairwell being held down. Matthews was able to receive sexual advantages simply because I am a survivor of sexual assault. I may never know how differently our relationship would have evolved if I were not damaged by the traumas of sexual assault but I do know that it's strengthening for me to talk about this as it takes away the stigma and the shame; I am a human being, someone who is capable of being duped.

It was another instance in which I was unaware of the reality of what was unfolding. Matthews was my friend and my lover, but he was also more than that—he was a lifeline for me in the Claims process; in fact, it's no exaggeration to say that without his help, I never would have filed the claim. And yet . . . what I could not acknowledge at the time was that in some way I was still allowing sex to be a factor in this military experience. It wasn't until years later that I began to consider the damage that I was inflicting on myself yet again by using sex as a tool during the Claims process.

When I submitted my claim to the VA, I expected that they would review my records, find out I was telling the truth, find my assailants and make them give me an apology, in addition to issuing a formal apology from the Air Force. You couldn't tell me that I was being naïve. I honestly expected the military to apologize for all the bad things that had happened, which ended my career in the Air Force. I fully expected that eventuality when my claim was approved. I was not prepared to be met with a period of silence for almost two years after my filing.

I remember Matthews asking sometime after the first year had passed if I had ever received a response, and I told him, "Nope, not a word."

He was shocked because he had known of someone else that he convinced to apply, and they had received a reply, so he told me to resubmit my claim or go down to the VA office and tell them what happened. I decided I was not going to go down there, so I resubmitted my claim online. I left it alone again and tried to go on living my life, but Matthews wouldn't leave it alone. He contacted me weeks later, and told me about a report that he had read about the backlog of cases at the Philadelphia VA and suggested that I contact my State Representative and request that they intercede on my behalf.

Once again, I did as I was told, I found out the name of my state representative and submitted an inquiry online requesting assistance. In retrospect, I think I was doing everything I could not have to go down to the VA directly. I don't know what I thought would happen to me if I had to go into their building. I think it was a kind of irrational fear that someone would pull me out of a line, point their finger at me, and yell, "LIAR! LIAR! Look at her! She's not a victim! How can she be a victim? Look at how perfectly combed her hair is and how well dressed she is as she comes sashaying her way up here to this office!"

I'd only seen victims on television, and they didn't seem to be well put together or collected. Sexual assault survivors on television always seemed to be helpless, devastated, and somehow sexually provocative at the same time.

These portraits seemed to be versions of what most people think "victims" look like in real life. But victimization looks different every single time because every single situation is different from all the others because there are so many ways to be violated. For example, in situations where the assault survivor knows her perpetrator, the attack could have happened during an innocent cup of coffee and progressed so quickly that it was over before the victim really had a chance to register what was going on. In a situation like that, one that does not involve a stranger, there may not have been any outwardly aggressive forms of violence outside of the rape itself. This is one reason why it is so important never to judge a survivor based on her experience alone because in many cases your version of the attack could be dead wrong.

I never received a reply from my state representative after my online submission or my faxed requests, but I did speak with another person at work who knew one of the councilmen in my district and he put me in touch with that person for possible assistance. The councilman sent me a form and asked me to complete it and send it back to his office, which I did, and once again I continued with my life.

Claim Lost... Now What?

A few months later, I received my first reply from Veterans Affairs. My heart sank, and I burst into tears. The form said they did not have a record of a formal submission and requested that I resubmit my claim in order to receive a reply. I was devastated. After every bit of two years, the first formal response I received was nothing more than a request that I resubmit my claim! It was maddening and I felt hopeless. I almost gave up right then and there, but once I told Matthews about the letter I received, he calmed me down.

"Don't get upset," he said, "just resubmit and this time go down to their office like I told you before and when you give them your submission, they'll stamp everything, make a copy and give you back your original documents."

Just like a good student, I did as I was told and scheduled a day off work so I could take the forms down there. Just driving up to the Veterans Administration office was a whole experience for me because once again I had all these irrational thoughts. On the drive, I drifted between thinking I would be stopped at the gate and not allowed to enter, to believe that once I entered the building I would be interrogated about my experiences before they would let me file. Victimization can make you irrational about normal daily occurrences.

The sun was shining bright in the clear blue sky and there was a slight breeze coming in through my windows as I pulled onto the grounds of the VA building. I had to stop at the booth before driving all the way onto their lot. The guard in the booth requested my identification and asked about my reason for visiting the VA that day. I searched in my purse for my driver's license, handed it to him, and told him that I was there to submit a claim. He told me where to park and pointed to the main entrance.

As I approached the entrance, I could see through the window the Security apparatus with guards in place and scanners. I followed the guard's instructions and proceeded through the body scanner. I was questioned again about why I was visiting the VA today. I then informed that officer that I was there to file a claim. It was a short walk to the claim's submission counter, where a woman gave me a form and asked me to fill it out. I took a seat at a table and I was grateful to be alone because I suddenly noticed that as I was filling out the form I was silently crying as I tried to put down everything about my assaults as succinctly as possible. It was extremely difficult to try to condense it all in a block of white space on a single sheet, front and back. After a few moments the woman called me back up to the desk, and as I tried to explain my challenge, she quickly shushed me.

"Just give me the paper," she said. "All you have to do is sign and date it. We'll find everything in your record and get back to you."

She turned to copy the form but then turned back. "Do you have any other documents to include with the form?" I gave her my copy of the dated/time-stamped submission I'd made years ago. She returned in a few minutes with my original and a copy of the completed form. I left the office, got back in my car, and drove home, mission accomplished.

After the re-submission, I expected things to really start moving along, but that wasn't the case. In September 2015, I received one of the first letters from the Department of Veterans Affairs, which informed me that they were still working on my claim and apologizing for the delay. It had been almost a year and a half and all I had was a standard form letter telling me to sit tight. I decided I could wait because I had already waited over two years with no information whatsoever, and now that I had resubmitted my claim it would be like starting the filing all over again.

But then I decided to take one more step and contact the head of all the Veterans Affairs offices, so I sent her a letter. There had been a recent personnel change at the VA, so I found the contact information online and submitted another letter electronically. At this point, I was emotionally detached from the filing, so I was able to behave just a bit more proactively in my quest for a response. The next time I decided to follow up on my claim, I didn't need Matthews to prompt me; I decided to do so on my own.

I also submitted an inquiry online to the Pennsylvania Governor's office. Once those two inquiries were submitted, things began to move. I received a communication that my case had been forwarded to the rating board for a decision. I was on fire now trying to think of who else I could contact for assistance and then it hit me. I had heard of people sending letters to President Obama requesting assistance with one issue or another so I decided that I might as well give that a try also. I went on Whitehouse.gov and submitted an inquiry.

Soon after, I received a form letter from the Department of Veterans Affairs thanking me for my "service to our country" and informing me that the letter was in response to my letter to President Obama concerning the status of my claim for service-connected compensation. The letter went on to state that "a thorough review of your file was completed, and we determined that your claim is ready for decision." I didn't know exactly what those words meant but at least I had finally received communication that was much more informative and definitive.

Apology- No, Apology

After submitting the claim at the VA office for the second time, per their request, and submitting the other additional inquiries, I resumed my life, going to work, then home to take care of the kids, and then back at it again, day after day. A significant amount of time passed, months, but then I finally received a demand from the VA to appear for a psychiatric evaluation related to my claim. Naturally, I conferred with Matthews again because I had no idea what to expect from the interview, how to prepare, nor did I know how to get to the VA hospital. Matthews was ecstatic for me that I was finally getting closer. He told me that my getting an interview meant that they had already researched my claim, determined that they were going to approve me for my claim and that the interview would be used to establish my disability rating percentage.

I needed him to slow down and repeat what he said because I couldn't understand how things had moved so slowly up to now, and then were suddenly speeding up. Up to this point, I really had no idea what the result would be of my filing. I was hoping for some sort of formal letter of apology and had no knowledge of disability percentages and ratings. Matthews explained that this whole process was all about leading towards a disability rating that would determine how much money I would receive from the military on a monthly basis. Once Matthews said those words to me, I dissolved into a long crying jag and then instantly got angry.

"WHERE IS MY APOLOGY? I want an apology!" I yelled.

Matthews looked me square in the face and grabbed me by my shoulders. "You ain't getting no apology from the military. The military will not give you an apology; all they can do is give you a monthly payment tied to a specific disability rating related to the disabilities that you possess as a result of your military experiences."

Matthews had to repeat those words several times before I was able to digest them and then once I could make sense of them, I started crying all over again.

"I don't care about the money!" I said. "What good is money going to do me now? They ruined my life! I could have had a career in the military, and my life would have turned out totally different. I know that if I had stayed in the military, I would have attained one higher rank after the other, completed my education years earlier, gotten married, and had a very good life. I was certain at the time that that would have been my path in the Air Force."

The CDC, Centers for Disease Control and Prevention, estimates that the economic burden of rape, per victim, is approximately $122,461. This calculation only takes into consideration those costs associated with receiving treatment and investigation. Those costs can never speak to the potential loss of income over a lifetime, unattained academic degrees, or generational losses due to the negative impact on our personal lives.

I believe that there is really no mathematical calculation that could ever come even close to reimbursing me for every road not taken as a direct result of being victimized during my time of military service. My life path was irrevocably altered and as a result there is no telling what I might have accomplished or even what image I would see reflected back at me when I look in the mirror.

Finally, I calmed down a bit and then asked Matthews to tell me again about what to expect from the psychological evaluation, how to get to the VA, and where to park. I ended the evening by having a tall cup of vodka and orange juice, sitting, and watching old Westerns in black and white, and then going home to bed after a couple of hours with Matthews.

The day of my psychological appointment arrived. I left work early and, following Matthews's instructions, I traveled down to the VA. I do not remember what floor my appointment was on but once inside the building I showed my appointment letter to one of the guards in the booth at the North entrance and they directed me where to go upstairs. I remembered being extremely nervous riding the elevator up, walking over to the desk, telling the lady at the desk why I was there, and then being instructed to have a seat. A little bit of time passed; I don't recall how much time but suddenly I heard my name being called from afar. I had drifted into a daze and had to bring myself back.

I was met by a male doctor in a white lab coat. He had black hair, a pink complexion, and was wearing a beige shirt with tan pants and black shoes. As he walked, his back was slightly to me and he turned toward me as we walked so, he could address me. I barely listened to what he said but I knew he was explaining a little bit about what was going to happen. We arrived at his office, a little room with a computer, and a dark-colored desk with books and papers strewn about. There was also a wooden coat rack in one corner off to my right side and a single empty chair facing his desk, and he motioned for me to sit there.

After we sat down, he restated his name and the purpose of the evaluation, telling me that he would make a report and send it to the VA. He explained that he did not work for the VA but that he was a contractor available on-site to conduct evaluations for the VA. I know that I responded verbally and nodded in response to his, but I literally could not hear my own voice or his. It was as if there were pillows over both of my ears and the sound was muffled as a way of softening the experience for me so that I could try to remain as calm as possible.

I could tell that he was good at his job because of the amount of time he took with me, coaxing me along with the retelling of my experiences. I remember feeling outside of myself and seeing my body make movements in concert with my verbal responses but to this day I still cannot see the experience any other way than as if it were a dream. I know that I spent a lot of the interview crying and that he calmed me down time after time so he could ask all his questions.

As I was answering a question about the physical rape itself, the light in the office suddenly went out and when it came back on, I was pushed up against the tall filing cabinet that was positioned in the office directly behind my chair. The light going off startled me so much that I felt as if I was lying back on that cot once again, unable to move and unable to cry out for help. I was shaking and crying all at once and having trouble breathing. I noticed the doctor appeared to be uncomfortable, but he recovered quickly and said a few words to help me calm down. He announced that we were almost done with the examination, asked a few more innocent questions just about logistics and the timeline, and then concluded the interview.

I gathered my belongings, thanked him for his time, and left the office still a bit shaken but also a bit lightheaded. As I walked back to my car, I noticed the chill in the air and the way the leaves were blowing on the pavement, just swirling, and swirling around from the wind. The more I walked, the calmer I became and by the time I had arrived back at my car, there was just the faintest bit of a smile on my face – I had made it through and came out the other side none the worse for wear. I told myself that maybe this was a sign things would get better for me.

I started to become curious about the VA disability ratings and visited the VA website to find out as much information as I could about what a disability rating would mean for me. I wondered how this rating would affect my ability to perform my job. Would they say that I suffered so much that I could no longer work and if so, how would I support my children and myself? I had many unanswered questions.

DETERMINATION-DISABLED

A short while later, maybe a few weeks, I received another letter from the VA. This time they were requesting that I attend another examination to assist with my disability rating. I had no idea what happened to the other report that the male doctor filed but this appointment was with a female psychiatrist and she was employed by the VA. This visit went just a little bit better than the last visit because this doctor was very good about helping to shield me from the most difficult parts of my retelling so that I wouldn't get overly emotional. She told me at the end of the examination that she didn't see any point in having me relive those painful experiences again and that she was able to gather all the information she needed without those recollections. She was very nice and even reassured me after our meeting that she was going to submit her recommendation for disability soon and that I should hear something in a short while.

On May 7th, more than 2 years after the resubmission, I was sitting at home running through my finances and checking my balance against the balance held on account with my credit union. I clicked submit after inputting my login ID and password, and I started crying and blinking my eyes rapidly wondering what in the world was going on. There was a large lump sum deposit sitting in my account followed by another separate deposit of a much smaller amount.

As I was guessing that this must be a mistake, I was also dialing Matthews's phone and waiting frantically for him to answer. He answered the phone in his usual jovial manner and since I was so choked up with tears, he pretty much guessed what I was trying to say. He told me to calm down and tell him how much I received. When I told him, he let out a long, slow whistle and said, "Damn girl, you rich!" Then he started laughing asking me why I was so shocked.

I explained that I had not received any mail from the VA, so I wasn't sure what was going on. He then told me that he had always known that this is what would happen, I would receive an automatic deposit into my bank account long before I ever received a notification in the mail. Here we go again, the VA, late as usual.

I told Matthews that I wasn't touching that money until I received some sort of mail from the VA. He told me that there was a number I could call if I wanted to and they would just tell me over the phone what had transpired. I told him I didn't need the number. I am fine just waiting it out and then I hung up the phone and sat there rocking back and forth trying to self-soothe after being shaken up like that so rudely. I ask myself the question now, years later, who but Berthienna, would be upset by receiving a large sum of money, money that I desperately needed mind you, in her bank account? I answered myself with a big fat... No one but you, silly. I know with certainty that practically anyone else would be running to the bank with a quickness to withdraw that money or just run to the stores buying up all kinds of stuff that my children definitely needed during that time.

When my mail was delivered later that afternoon, there in the mailbox was a medium-sized, manila envelope labeled U. S. Department of Veterans Affairs. The VA had made the determination of disability for "Post Traumatic Stress Disorder (PTSD) with alcohol use disorder due to military sexual trauma, also claimed as anxiety, depression, panic attacks, and sleep disorder" and given me a disability rating with an effective date from two years earlier.

As I read on the explanation continued stating that my rating was based on the following:

*Difficulty in adapting to stressful circumstances

*Difficulty in adapting to work
*Suspiciousness
*Depressed mood
*Suicidal ideation
*Disturbances of motivation and mood
*Difficulty in adapting to a work-like setting
*Anxiety
*Difficulty in establishing and maintaining effective work and social relationships
*Chronic sleep impairment
*Panic attacks more than once a week
*Occupational and social impairment with reduced reliability and productivity.

After reading the complete evaluation of my determination of disability, I broke down crying yet again because it was like seeing confirmation of the fact that I was broken. The military took a little, naïve teenager from the big, bad, bold streets of North Philadelphia and broke her spirit. I was not crazy. I am not crazy after all. I had just been beaten up by life situations and yet I still stood ready to be the protector that my children needed to grow up in this world.

Once I adjusted and wrapped my head around the disability determination, I had to figure out what to do with the money. At the time I felt like it was dirty money: I felt the way I imagined survivors must have felt in the past when they were abused by big, rude men or big, bad companies and they were then given compensation and told to just go away and keep their mouths shut. It took a while for me to feel like it was okay to spend the money. I didn't even tell my children about the money right away.

As I began to spend money on them and the house, whenever they would ask where the money came from, I would just tell them that I had cashed in some savings bonds that I had forgotten about. That explanation seemed to quiet everyone down for quite a while but at a certain point, my eldest daughter and son came to me separately with similar questions. Basically, they said that they could believe some of the money came from savings bonds but not all of it and they wanted to know the truth. I told them that the money came from the VA for my time in the service. It was just that simple. They didn't dig too hard into the why of it, they just let my explanation fly. I couldn't believe how easy it was to withhold the full truth about the money. I was not yet at the point where I could tell them about being assaulted in the military, so I told a variation of the truth.

Six months or so after the initial payment and the deposits were coming in every month, Matthews contacted me again and asked me if I had submitted a request to the VA for the adjustment. I didn't know what he was talking about so he reminded me that he remembered that my determination was effective dated a full two years AFTER my original filing, so the VA owed me additional compensation.

I listened and then pulled out my determination letter again and it turns out that Matthews was right again. There, in black and white, was the effective date based upon my second filing date and not the original filing date so I was owed additional compensation from the date of the initial filing two years prior. Man, that Matthews was quite a good friend to have in my life during those difficult times.

Matthews walked me through the process of requesting the adjustment and I filed another form and waited. Communication went back and forth between me and the VA for another year and finally I received the decision from the reviewing officer that "entitlement to an earlier effective date for service connection of posttraumatic stress disorder with alcohol use disorder due to military sexual trauma also claimed as anxiety, depression, panic attacks, and sleep disorder is granted because a clear and unmistakable error was made therefore, a new effective date has been assigned."

I COUNT THE DARK

As a result of that decision, I received another lump sum deposit in my account and the monthly payment was increased as well due to the standard cost of living increases that veterans are normally granted.

Military Sexual Trauma-MST

As you might imagine, I cried again, but this time they weren't tears of incredulity but tears of gratitude that my initial submission was finally recognized. All of the hard work that I endured within this process finally led to a conclusion, and everything turned out well. Over the course of the next few years, I communicated with the VA to add my children to my claim status, verify the type of medical and psychological coverage that I would receive, and determine my eligibility for many other types of benefits.

As a citizen of Philadelphia and a veteran, before this process began, I never knew there was a VA office in Philadelphia, much less that any veteran could go there for services and discussion of compensation claims. As I think back on this entire process, I reflect on the doubt, fear, and anxiety that I felt all along the way. I would have stopped numerous times along this road had it not been for my friend Matthews. I know from the many conversations I've had with the female veterans that participate in the Military Sexual Trauma meetings that most of them have their claims denied repeatedly and most of them give up after the first attempt. It is a testament to how hard it is to go up against any big entity and most especially a governmental entity like the United States Military.

I know how truly blessed I am that I had a friend like Matthews because not everyone has someone in their corner urging them to keep trying and not to give up. Yes, I had my family in my corner but at the time I was unable to disclose my experiences to them so there was only so much they were able to do for me. As I sit in one MST meeting after the other, continuing to listen to the shared experiences of other military personnel, active-duty, reserve, and veterans alike, I listen carefully to the shares about denials for compensation and the difficulties these women face daily as they try to make their way through the complicated compensation process. I make sure to stay after the meeting is over to share my experiences with those women in hopes that it will help someone on their road to a positive determination.

I also think about the almost five years I spent engaged in the process and the number of times that I quit, just plain stopped trying, because I was weary of all the setbacks and I felt like the military was never, ever going to see me, hear me and believe me. I don't know where I would be today if I had listened to myself and not heeded the well-meaning advice of my friend Matthews. I am thankful that he kept telling me to push on and don't stop until you receive every consideration owed for the hurt inflicted upon me during my time of service. All in all, his friendship has meant a lot to me over the years. I know that I would have given up years ago were it not for his constant encouragement to keep pushing on no matter how long it takes. I was a patron of giving up at the slightest nudge because of how easy it was to just give in back then rather than fight my battles. I can look back on my trials and tribulations now and acknowledge that perseverance is my seed and it is deeply rooted within me.

Once my claim was submitted and in process, I began to receive services for Military Sexual Assault and because of receiving this service, I could see a VA psychiatrist for treatment. I credit the staff at the VA hospital with my current level of recovery and the many years spent trying to figure out all this stuff on my own while working with other primary care physicians. The irony in coming full circle, as it were, is not lost on me in this retelling of a big chapter in my life. My life was turned upside down while serving in the military and here now after many years have passed, I reached out to the VA for help and assistance with turning my life right-side-up again. A clear example of 'holding onto God's unchanging hands.'

During, the course of my life, I find it horrifying the number of times I have experienced sexual assault, attempted rape, rape by a former sexual partner, and mental abuse at the hands of different men. I often wondered if I had the words, "SUCKER…COME GET ME…VICTIM IN NEED OF SOMEONE TO SEXUALLY ASSAULT ME!" or some other equally vile and nonsensical words tattooed on my forehead, but of course, that's just too stupid to fathom.

Military Sexual Trauma–As Defined By The Va

As we can tell by the many reports popping up in the news, time is still not on a woman's side when it comes to recollecting acts of violence and abuse and looking for the perpetrators to be prosecuted accordingly. All one has to do is look at the many prevailing narratives in the press of case after case of sexual assault, rape, and domestic abuse and we can clearly see that time has not been kind to women in situations such as these.

For the most part, the assumption is made that the woman somehow misjudged the situation and nothing untoward happened at the moment; therefore, no charges are filed and if/or when charges are filed, they are typically summarily dismissed and mentioned in a very small postscript in the newspaper or digital media. A postscript that is most often very hard to find unless you are scouring through newspapers daily looking for a mention. Well, things are not so very different today than they were back in the 1980s.

Anu Bhagwati, the Executive Director of SWAN-Service Women's Action Network, and a form Marine Corps Captain, said the following: "So let us be clear. Rape and assault are violent, traumatic crimes, not mistakes, not lapses of professional judgment, not leadership failures, and not oversights in character. Rape is about power, control, and intimidation." She went on to state that "the DOD (Department of Defense) itself estimates that 19,300 assaults occurred in 2010, and that while 8,600 victims were female, 10,700 were male."

Since 2010, the military has noticed the rise in purported cases of Sexual Assaults with the percentages increasing from 38% to 40% or more in the last decade alone. An article from *The New York Times* (May 2, 2019) stated that *"Women now make up only about 20 percent of the military, but are the targets of 63 percent of assaults, the survey found, with the youngest and lowest-ranking women most at risk."*

Let's pause here a moment and define what has been identified by the Department of Veterans Affairs as Military Sexual Trauma and Sexual Assault as listed on the PTSD.gov website: "The definition used by the VA comes from Federal law (Title 38 U.S. Code 1720D) and is as follows: "psychological trauma, which in the judgement of a VA mental health professional, resulted from a physical assault of a sexual nature, battery of a sexual nature, or sexual harassment which occurred while the Veteran was serving on active duty, active duty training, or inactive duty training." . . . "Sexual harassment is further defined as "repeated, unsolicited verbal or physical contact of a sexual nature which is threatening in character." The harassment that I suffered during my time of service was repeated several times over by male service members holding the rank of Sgt and higher. The word of an AIC simply did not have as much weight as that of a Sgt, SSgt, TSgt or above at that time in the military. It is highly likely that their gender as well as their rank played a part in my treatment following the disclosure of harassment that I was subjected to during my time of service.

Sexual Harassment and the UCMJ

In the news as of late we have become more aware of horrific instances of sexual abuse, sexual assault, and in a few cases, even murder, purportedly committed by male military personnel against female military personnel. The recent death of US Army Specialist Vanessa Guillén, in August of 2020, sparked a movement in the military reminiscent of the #MeToo movement spearheaded by Tarana Burke. Guillén, who was bludgeoned to death, feared her claims of sexual harassment would not be believed, so she never reported her claims of sexual harassment.

In 2020, the #IAmVanessaGuillen bill, HR 8270 (116th Congress) was signed into law, one main tenet of the bill focused on making Sexual Harassment a crime included within the Uniform Code of Military Justice (UCMJ). Among the many loud voices clamoring for changes in how sexual assault claims are handled in the military, I have zeroed in on the voice of Senator Kristen Gillibrand, Democrat, New York. In addition to HR 8270, there is another bill being put up before the committee for consideration, HR 4104-Vanessa Guillén Military Justice Improvement, and Increasing Prevention Act. This bill and several others, if voted into law, will change the face of how sexual assault is handled in the military by making it easier to report claims of sexual assault without fear of recrimination. In the past as well as presently, many victims chose not to report their claims simple because they feel uncomfortable reporting claims within the same chain-of-command shared by their purported perpetrator. It is my belief that until the military begins to fully see the benefits of having these cases reviewed by independent lawyers and consultants, it will continue to miss the mark on bringing about the justice that so many victims and survivors of military sexual assault endure on a daily basis.

As recently as February 4, 2021, a news report was released concerning allegations of Rape and Sexual Assault at Fort Campbell (Kentucky-Tennessee). A WSMV News4 investigator is quoted in this article as saying, "These soldiers ultimately say – if you report a rape, it's likely going to end your career." The more I looked around, the more aware I became of the fact that sexual assault in the military is just as rampant today, if not more so, than it was during my time of service. It was around this time that I took a decisive step toward advocacy following the reading of yet another article in *The Washington Post* (June 28, 2012), that chronicled a sexual abuse scandal purportedly at Lackland AFB, San Antonio, Texas. The article spoke about a number of Training Instructors (T.I's) at Lackland AFB who were being charged with sexual abuse of training recruits. Although my abuse did not happen at Lackland AFB, the article brought to light the fact that 33 years later airmen were still being assaulted and raped under the command of their superior officers and training instructors. Shortly after that story came out, I started becoming aware of many other stories being published about sexual abuse in the military. As these stories became more widespread, I started having flashbacks to the sexual assaults that I experienced in the military.

Past... Present... Future

If we go back 40 years or more, it is easy to imagine that the story about Lackland AFB is my story-my career was effectively ended following my rape and sexual assaults, which was also compounded by the deaths in my family at the time.

When I think back on that incident it brings into sharp focus the sexual attacks committed against women and children today. Are things really any different today? SSgt Davis and Sgt Berlmont were relocated in the same way that pedophile priests are relocated by the Catholic Church for their bad deeds. The military was and is just as guilty of covering up incidences of sex crimes and all other manners of military sexual trauma (MST). MST has become a huge problem for the military, so much so that they have formed teams and groups in Veterans Administration hospitals where the veterans and active-duty personnel can meet to develop skills and discuss treatment options for MST. I have personally heard many stories of women young and old, active-duty, reservists, and veterans, of their experiences in the past and present where they were simply not believed or not treated fairly by the military.

Mama Ruth, with all her good intentions, could never have imagined that the place she thought could be a refuge from harm for me actually turning out to be more harmful than staying in North Philly and having babies would have been. Back in Philly, I knew Mama Ruth was there to protect me from harm, along with all my brothers, sisters, and Davis. If I had stayed, I imagine Davis and I would have been married and started a family. Let me propose a question here for consideration. *Do you believe that the average 19-year-*

old can really manage a state of independence navigating the world on her(his) own? I think not. Nineteen is too young to really know and experience how cruel the world can be to a young airman. I know now that those assaults brought about feelings of distrust of men, men in positions of authority, as well as distrust of institutions and governments holding positions of authority over me.

This is part and parcel of what haunts me so much in regard to my ordeals: the scars of shame, humiliation, worthlessness, and despair that I suffered through for years afterward. Then to have all of those years summed up into a financial award with the stigma of 'disability' attached to it, naturally, did not leave me in a good place. I effectively went from being an unseen and unheard 'victim' to another type of 'victim' one that is much more acceptable in society – the disabled.

I do not believe that we, society, can effectively explain what makes one person more susceptible to being victimized than another and even if there was an explanation, I don't know if I could believe it because 'victimization' seems to just happen, most times without warning. It is not planned. I definitely did not wake up one morning and decide that I wanted to be victimized today. I can tell you that I did wake up one morning deciding that I would no longer be a victim of anyone's anger, rage, or selfish desires.

If I had to come up with one reason for my survival, I can only say that it is because of my faith in God, the strength given to me by my mother, and the words spoken to me over and over again, by her mother, my grandmother BerthaMae Ford. BerthaMae always told me to "Be Ready when God calls and **always, always,** hold on to his unchanging hands". If I had given up as I wanted to do on many different occasions, I know for a fact that I would not have my four beautiful children, I would never have been married and I would never have experienced true love and friendship from the many people that have touched my life.

BEACON OF LIGHT

Today, we are experiencing the benefits of the light shone on sexual assault/abuse and rape brought about by the #MeToo movement by way of its founder, Tarana Burke. This light is long overdue and it is my hope that it shines brightly forever more but forgive me if I think the 'light' will one day dim again and we will find ourselves no further away from this form of abuse than we were when it all began.

It is my opinion that the only way we can help sustain this 'beacon of light' is by taking the time to design and implement new laws like HR 8270, the #IAmVanessaGuillén bill, HR 4104-Vanessa Guillén Military Justice Improvement and Increasing Prevention Act, and others that have yet to be proposed, to protect victims moving forward. I am also a firm believer in reviewing the statute of limitation laws that exist for sexual abuse cases in light of the fact that individuals that sustain PTSD related to sexual assault traumas, may not have recollections of their abuse until many years after the attack has taken place.

Over the course of my lifetime, I have spiraled out of control many times only to find myself right-side up after years of fighting myself and my demons. As women, we owe it to ourselves, our daughters, our nieces, our sisters, and our sistahs, to always stand up for one another, to help lift each other up, to stand whenever one of us finds ourselves incapable of standing, to hug each other, to cry with and for one another, collectively as well as singularly. We owe it to each other to shout loudly and forcefully, craving justice for one another whenever anyone of us suffers abuse. We owe it to one another to let our voices be heard on the floor of Congress as we fight for new laws to be implemented and old laws to be reviewed, revised, and even demolished, as necessary, so that we can break the boulders of sexual abuse/assault and rape. Let the mightiest hammer of our collective voices serve to smash the boulders finally reducing them to rubble and from there to dust that can be easily blown away into nothingness. I believe that if we can do this that we will one day live in a space where the reality of Sexual Assault/Abuse and Rape are no longer perceived as the type of crime that is often unreported out of fear of reprisal, shame, humiliation or one that is accepted as normal behavior as it is in some countries like Afghanistan where women know that the likelihood of being raped is a surety just by nature of the fact that they were born female.

1979 to 2022, Change happens slowly…

We are dealing with the reality that the military has no better means of handling reports of rape and sexual assault back in the early 1980s than it does today. The only thing that appears to be different on the surface is the year is 2022 and not 1980. There is another equally shameful reality in my opinion, and that is thus: the sheer number of unknown cases of rape and sexual assault that occurred in every branch of the military from the moment women were granted permission to serve alongside our male counterparts will never be known. I cannot imagine what manner of abuse and shame women were subjected to back then, nor do I have the strength at this time to go down that path of pain, anger, resentment, humiliation, and shame. However, I do feel that I must stand in the gap as a representative for my fellow airman/soldiers to let them know that their collective voices are FINALLY being heard.

As I sit today, I am most grateful for the long shadow being cast which has taken us through the trials of Bill Cosby and Harvey Weinstein ushering in a form of healing and therapy allowing some victims to move forward with their lives. Many question if justice has been served in these trials; however, I feel certain that if you ask any victim about 'justice being served', you will hear the word 'NO' more often than not, as there is really no measure of 'justice' that can heal a victim of sexual assault/abuse and/or rape. The scars of sexual assault trauma are never fully eradicated; however, through time and in conjunction with many healing practices, both medicinal and holistic, I believe we can significantly reduce the ill effects caused by how trauma is displayed in our lives.

In my journey of life, I have stumbled and paused, I have had many false starts and many missteps along the way and as I am about to approach my 63rd year of blessings, I am proud to say that now my steps are strong and stable, walking with a level of assurance and joy that I have truly never felt before now.

I have been blessed in my life to finally re-connect with my very first friend from Basic Military Training School, Myra Neely, nee Ratchford. Myra or "Mykee" as she was affectionately known back then, and I share the very same birthday, June 28th and that was the basis for the beginning of our friendship back then.

Mykee found me through social media in 2019 and surprised me with a phone call that I will never forget. I vividly recall how emotional we both became during that initial phone call, crying tears of joy mixed with wonder as we tried to catch up on so much lost time. Unfortunately, we lost touch not long afterwards; however, she persevered and found me yet again in 2021. That was one of the best manifestations of perseverance that I have experienced in my life.

Although we have both advanced in age, lived experiences, our friendship and love for one another never subsided. It is almost as if our bond was placed in a time capsule just waiting for such as time as this to be opened. We've flown across the country several times, sharing laughter, and creating new memories as our friendship has grown stronger and stronger on an entirely new level.

I am now more at peace and settled as a mother of four beautiful children, a sister to six siblings (two deceased but never forgotten), a friend to many, and the proud daughter of one beautifully, audacious human being, RuthieMae.

Over the course of these past 42 plus years, I have leaned on many friends, family members and professionals to help me make it this far. I learned with the help of many psychiatrists, psychologists, therapists, and all other manners of mental health professionals, that I am a woman worthy of respect and love. So, as you take my story with you in your lives, I want to encourage women everywhere to speak out, speak up and reach up for help from any and every source possible to heal yourself from the ravages of mental, physical, and sexual abuse because... *I Count the Dark*, and I know that even in the 'dark', which is sometimes a cold and lonely place; that if you just hold on a little while longer, you too can find yourself.

I Count The Dark

A Poem

dominating, besetting, gripping me to a point of ICE…

urgent, riveting, standing there in the glow silently simmering while trying not to EXPLODE…

it's messy, chaotic, full of blurred lines … reminding me of what it feels like to be sliced, TWICE!

what is missing? what am i owed? is it that they want me to IMPLODE?

as a child i sang….5, 6, 7, 8, who do we appreciate….

and 3, 6, 9, the goose drank wine

Mmmm wine.. so much so that i saw myself shrinking smaller and smaller down into nothingness and beyond.

how do i ground me you say? How do I stay present when I go to those places that don't keep me here? i count!

i count the spaces, the places, the faces, the races, the paces.

i count until i erase all sense of time…… i count the light until finally i am left with nothing left to count – so i count the dark.

arithmomania…. ocd…. sounds like tomato – tomatoe to me.

So, Yes,

I COUNT THE DARK

I Count The Dark
REFERENCES-WEBSITE SOURCES:

"Abuse Survivors Can Be Revictimized — Here's What You Should Know." Healthline.Com. December 16, 2020. https://www.healthline.com/health/revictimization#the-role-of-stigma.

"Air Force Investigates Growing Sex Abuse Scandal." Washington Post. June 28, 2012. https://www.washingtonpost.com/world/national-%20security/air-force-investigates-growing-sex-abusescandal/2012/06/28/gJQAutm39V_story.html?noredirect=o%20n&utm_term=.5408f1eb31a6.

Cividanes GC, Mello AF, Mello MF. Revictimization as a high-risk factor for development of posttraumatic stress disorder: a systematic review of the literature. Braz J Psychiatry. 2019 Jan-Feb;41(1):82-89. doi: 10.1590/1516-4446-2017-0013. Epub 2018 Oct 11. PMID: 30328955; PMCID: PMC6781702.

"The Cost of Rape." National Sexual Violence Resource Center. Pennsylvania Coalition Against Rape, December 4, 2018. https://www.nsvrc.org/blogs/cost-rape.

"Early Intervention with Eye Movement Desensitisation and Reprocessing (EMDR) Therapy to Reduce the Severity of Posttraumatic Stress Symptoms in Recent Rape Victims: Study Protocol for a Randomised Controlled Trial." Taylor & Francis. July 1, 2019. https://doi.org/10.1080/20008198.2019.1632021.

Info@Aapf.org. January 09, 2022. https://www.aapf.org/hdd-2016 1/9/2022

Info@Aapf.Org January 19, 2022. https://www.aapf.org/hdd.

"Kirstin Gillibrand U. S. Senator for New York." Kirstin Gillibrand. February 26, 2023. https://www.gillibrand.senate.gov/about.
Strategic Air Command. Accessed February 26, 2023. https://en.wikipedia.org/wiki/Strategic_Air_Command.

BERTHIENNA E. GREEN

About Berthienna E. Green

Author, Warrior-Writer Facilitator, Poet, Motivational Speaker, Wellness Coach and aspires to become an End-of Life Doula.

She is also a proud mother of 4, a grandmother of 4, an Air Force veteran, and a Survivor of Military Sexual Trauma. She will be launching a non-profit–ScreamingwithnoVoice, to focus on helping survivors of Sexual Assault, Domestic Abuse, Rape, and Attempted Suicide or as she has termed it… "**sui-DE-cided.**"

Berthienna stands firm in her belief that at her lowest moments the '**DEcision**' was **not** to end her life but rather to 'end' the pain. Unfortunately, in many cases the '**DEcisions** made in connection with the methods chosen may often result in a loss of life as was the case for her brother, James Wilson Green.

In Berthienna's heart she believed that in her attempts she would succeed in eradicating the pain, shame, humiliation, and self-blame from her daily existence and thereby emerge victorious moving forward into a life without suicidal ideations or further suicide attempts. This is where she has coined the phrase '**sui-DE-cided.**

Berthienna's life today is focused on doing whatever she can to assist in building up the self-confidence and self-esteem of survivors of Military Sexual Trauma/Rape/Sexual Violence, Attempted Suicide and Domestic Violence through listening to the testimonies of other survivors', the work through her nonprofit, ScreamingwithnoVOICE, facilitating writing workshops, motivational speaking and also the simple act of a smile, handshake, or a hug in hopes of helping thrivers everywhere live and lead lives of triumph free of suffering.

She has an Associates in Entrepreneurship and Small Business, a Bachelor's in Business Administration w/Management concentration, and a Certificate in Women's Entrepreneurship. She believes in continuing education and how important it is to *apply* the knowledge we have learned in life and let it move us closer on our journey toward better results in many areas of our lives.

She is a fearless woman of God and a lover of words. She is a woman who knows that with Perseverance-you can do a mighty big thing. Her foundation is: "Perseverance is MY seed. What's yours?"

If you are seeking a motivational, engaging, and lively speaker/facilitator for your next event, Berthienna is only a text, phone call, or email away. You may connect with her via email, cellular, and/or on her social media platforms.

FaceBook:
@Tina Green

Instagram:
@btina_6; @oswnv2022

Business websites:
berthiennaegreen.com
screamingwithnovoice.org

Email:
contact@screamingwithnovoice.org
info_921@berthiennaegreen.com
www.icountthedark.com

Cellular: **267-313-3311**

CPSIA information can be obtained
at www.ICGtesting.com
Printed in the USA
BVHW051303180423
662562BV00016BA/817